CITY IN TIME | Washington, D.C.

CITY IN TIME | **Washington, D.C.**

SAMUEL M. CAGGIULA WITH BEVERLEY BRACKETT

ORIGINAL PHOTOGRAPHY BY GILBERT KING

New York / London
www.sterlingpublishing.com

Library of Congress Cataloging-in-Publication Data

Caggiula, Samuel M.
City in time. Washington, D.C. / Samuel M. Caggiula with Beverley Brackett ; original photography by Gilbert King.
p. cm.
ISBN-13: 978-1-4027-3609-4
ISBN-10: 1-4027-3609-6
1. Washington (D.C.)--History. 2. Washington (D.C.)—Geography. 3. Washington (D.C.)—Pictorial works.
4. Historic buildings—Washington (D.C.) 5. Washington (D.C.)—Buildings, structures, etc.
I. Brackett, Beverley. II. King, Gilbert. III. Title. IV. Title: Washington, D.C.
F194.C24 2008
975.3--dc22
2007032575

10 9 8 7 6 5 4 3 2 1

Published by Sterling Publishing Co., Inc.
387 Park Avenue South, New York, NY 10016

Distributed in Canada by Sterling Publishing
c/o Canadian Manda Group, 165 Dufferin Street
Toronto, Ontario, Canada M6K 3H6
Distributed in the United Kingdom by GMC Distribution Services
Castle Place, 166 High Street, Lewes, East Sussex, England BN7 1XU
Distributed in Australia by Capricorn Link (Australia) Pty. Ltd.
P.O. Box 704, Windsor, NSW 2756, Australia

Design by 3+Co. (www.threeandco.com)

Many of the archival photographs featured in the City in Time series are more than
100 years old and have not been altered to conceal damage or wear from the effects of time.

Printed in China

Sterling ISBN-13: 978-1-4027-3609-4
ISBN-10: 1-4027-3609-6

For information about custom editions, special sales, and premium
and corporate purchases, please contact Sterling Special Sales
Department at 800-805-5489 or specialsales@sterlingpublishing.com.

Preface

We hope that this volume of the City in Time series will compel you first to wonder about, then appreciate, and ultimately better understand the development and achievements of the world's great urban centers. The series offers not only interesting time-lapsed juxtapositions, but also meaningful and contrasting images that shed light on the unique resources, circumstances, and creative forces that have propelled these cities to greatness. In a world where renovation and development are so often casually destructive, visual history can be a reservoir of wisdom from which we can inspire and refresh ourselves. We invite you to reflect upon the accomplishments of those who came before us and revel in these impressive monuments to human ambition.

Introduction

A New Country, a New City, a New Beginning

Shortly after being elected the first President of the United States, George Washington turned his attention to the establishment of a national capital city. In the end, the location of Washington, D.C., was decided upon as part of a political deal. Through the Revolutionary War, the central government had been located in Philadelphia. With the establishment of the nation's federal city below the Mason-Dixon Line, the representatives of southern states were appeased, feeling more connected to the overall leadership and control of the country. For their concession, northern state governments were relieved of their massive war debts.

This compromise was a smart move for the new country, as it helped create a national identity with a viewpoint that was leaning neither fully north nor fully south. The location that President George Washington selected for the capital in 1790 was a plot of land along the Potomac and the Anacostia Rivers, between the ports of Alexandria, Virginia, and Georgetown, Maryland—with both states giving up land for the new city. The nascent country of thirteen states was entering uncharted waters with a new system of government, a new electorate, and a new capital city. The country's early leaders—fresh from the success of winning the Revolutionary War—believed the future held the promise of growth and prosperity.

Even in its earliest plans, the city of Washington combined the rugged frontier concept of the American wilderness with a classic European design plan. Here was a city of dirt roads and marshland that was laid out to one day include great museums, stately residences, and institutions of higher learning. The name—Washington City in the District of Columbia—paid respect to both sides of the Atlantic as well, by honoring both George Washington and Christopher Columbus in one address.

The city grew from cow pastures and woodlands, and was fairly uncivilized for its first thirty years or so. Early congressmen were shocked at the deplorable living and working conditions when they arrived in the mud that later would become the National Mall. After the city was damaged during the War of 1812, repairs and new construction skyrocketed around the city. In time, advances in civil engineering turned marshland into the sites where the Lincoln Memorial and Ronald Reagan National Airport are now located.

The pages that follow show that as times and tastes changed, so too did the city. A few lucky buildings—Union Station, the Old Executive Building, and the Old Post—have been saved from planned demolition. While residential areas have come in and out of fashion, Dupont Circle and Georgetown are today two of the most highly desirable places to live.

Washington is a city in which the architectural styles are as varied as the political opinions. One need only to look at the extreme differences between the National Gallery East and West or the Lincoln Memorial and the Vietnam Veterans Memorial to see the stark contrasts. Washington, D.C., is a stunning city of contrasts and diversity that also inspires unity and pride in the nation.

From 1860 to 1935, the Supreme Court of the United States was housed on the second floor of the Capitol Building in the Old Senate Chamber. In 1935, the chief justice and eight associate justices moved into new quarters: an imposing neoclassical edifice designed by the architect Cass Gilbert. Built with marble from Vermont, Georgia, and Alabama, the building is reminiscent of a Greek temple, with steps leading up to a portico supported by Corinthian columns.

SUPREME COURT { PRESENT }

Those entering the building pass under a pediment decorated with nine allegorical figures including Liberty, Authority, and Order, and a lintel carved with the famous motto "Equal Justice Under Law." This principle—a touchstone of American law—holds the promise that those appearing in U.S. courts will receive fair hearings of their cases, regardless of their economic or social status. The Supreme Court has issued many decisions in keeping with that principle, some of which, while initially unpopular, have become landmarks of American constitutional law.

LIBRARY OF CONGRESS—THOMAS JEFFERSON BUILDING { PAST }

The Library of Congress opened on the rainy Monday morning of November 1, 1897. With its Beaux-Arts edifice resembling that of the Paris Opera House, the library was built to house and protect an ever-growing collection that had previously suffered two devastating fires. The varied and numerous artworks complementing the design of the domed Great Hall make it one of the most impressive spaces in the entire city. Though it has been considered the most beautiful and richly ornamented public building in the United States, the library actually opened under budget and ahead of schedule.

LIBRARY OF CONGRESS—THOMAS JEFFERSON BUILDING { PRESENT }

LORE & LEGEND

In addition to books, music, and other documents, the Library of Congress preserves rare and unusual artifacts like the contents of President Lincoln's pockets from the day he was assassinated and a collection of Stradivarius violins.

Renamed for its visionary in 1980, the Thomas Jefferson Building underwent extensive renovation starting in 1986, culminating with its centennial celebration in 1997. The world's largest library now includes two additional buildings: the John Adams Building and the James Madison Memorial Building. Together, they house more than 130 million items in 460 languages on approximately 530 miles of bookshelves, as well as the government's Copyright Office. In recent years, the National Digital Library Program has made much of the massive collection's information available over the Internet.

CAPITOL BUILDING { PAST }

Home to Congress—the legislative branch of the U.S. government—the Capitol Building sits atop land believed to have been originally used for meetings by two Algonquin tribes, the Manahoacs and Monacans. When it was first proposed as the location of the future Capitol Building, the site was actually in the middle of a swampy wilderness, as this photo from July 1861 illustrates. Today, it is the meeting ground of two very different tribes: the two elected bodies of the U.S. Congress—the Senate and House of Representatives.

CAPITOL BUILDING { PRESENT }

The Capitol features two wings: the south wing, home to the House of Representatives, and the north wing, home to the Senate. Not all congressional offices are located within the Capitol, though. A maze of underground tunnels connects the Capitol with neighboring office buildings. The Capitol's most recognizable feature, however, is its central Rotunda. The District is divided into quadrants (SW, NW, NE, SE) named for their location in relation to the Rotunda. On July 4, tens of thousands of people gather on Capitol Hill to celebrate the nation's birthday with music and a grand display of fireworks.

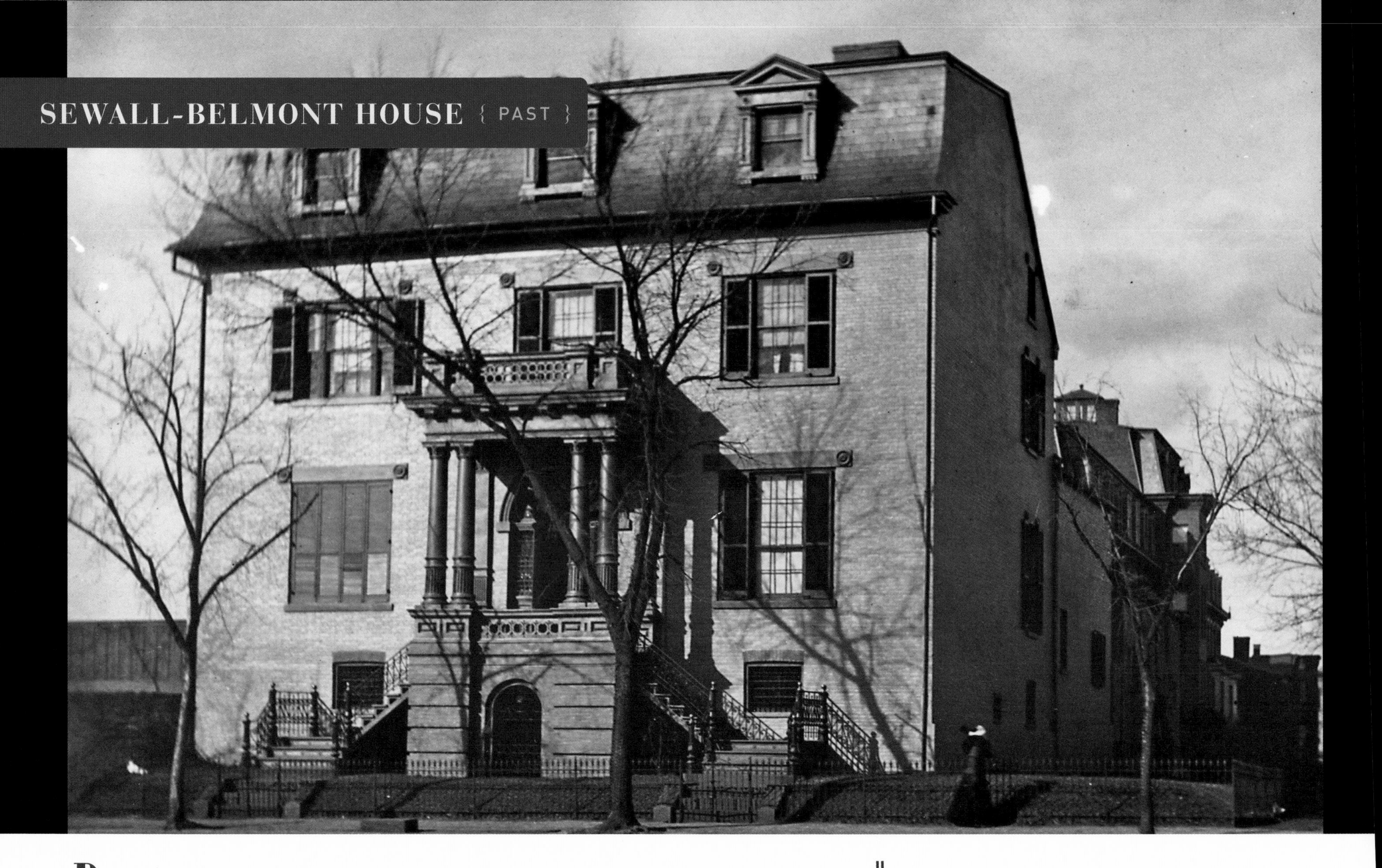

SEWALL-BELMONT HOUSE { PAST }

Built by Robert Sewall in 1800, the Sewall-Belmont House is one of the oldest once-residential properties still standing on Capitol Hill. One of the earliest tenants of this gracious brick house was Albert Gallatin, the Secretary of Treasury under Presidents Jefferson and Madison. Some sources claim the Sewall-Belmont House is where the details and financial arrangements of the Louisiana Purchase were ironed out. The house adapted and changed with the styles of different periods but stayed in the Sewall family for more than 120 years.

SEWALL-BELMONT HOUSE { PRESENT }

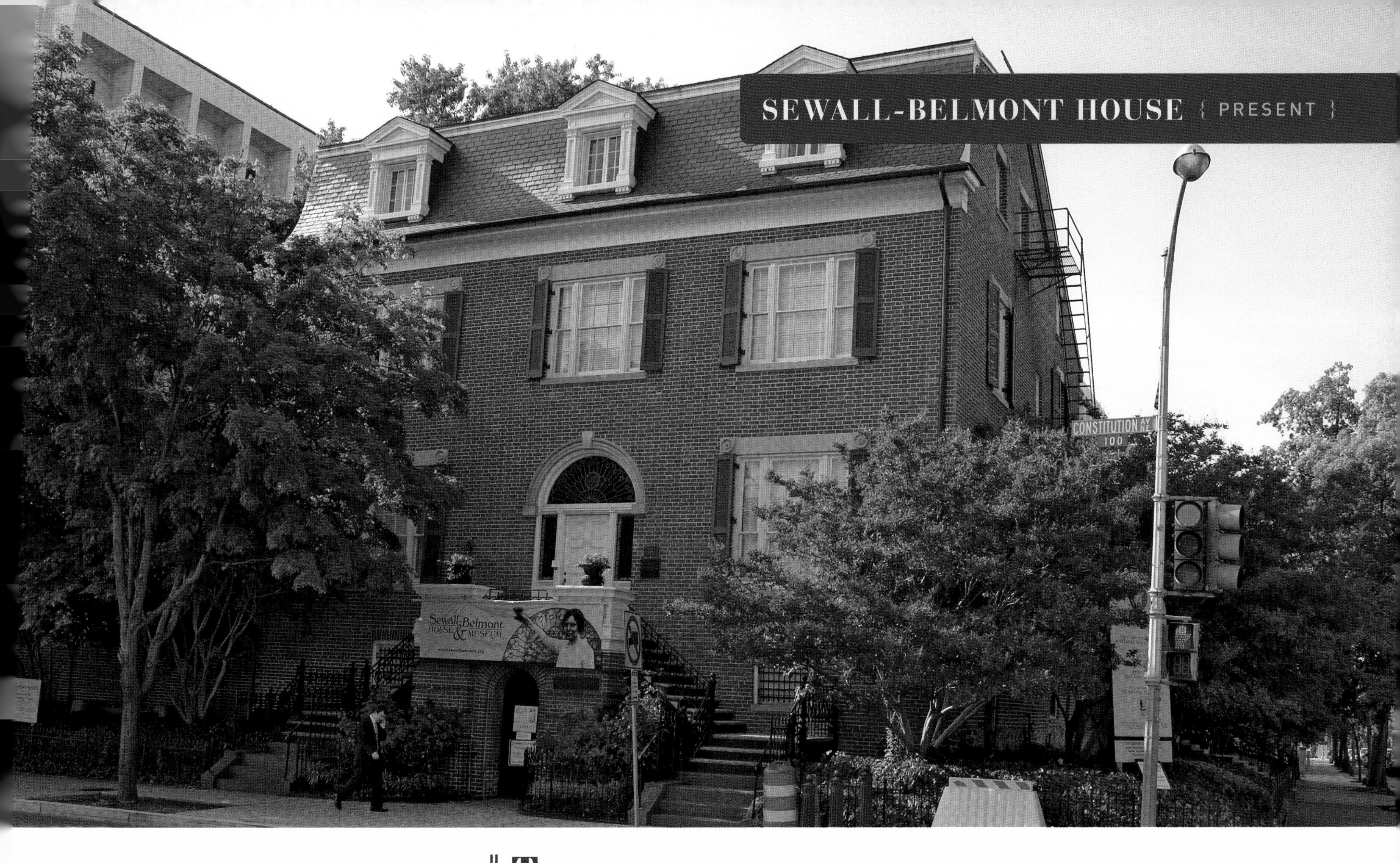

The Sewall-Belmont House has been a center of political activity in Washington for more than 200 years. Now a National Historic Landmark, the house serves as a museum and the headquarters for the National Woman's Party, which purchased the house in 1929. This party and its dynamic leader, Alice Paul, were instrumental in getting the 19th Amendment, which granted women the right to vote, ratified in 1920. The museum presents the history of women's suffrage in this country and even houses a desk that once belonged to women's rights leader Susan B. Anthony.

NATIONAL MALL { PAST }

Part of Pierre L'Enfant's original plans for the city, the National Mall stretches two and a half miles, from the Capitol Building down to the banks of the Potomac River. L'Enfant envisioned the Mall as a green space lined by Parisian-style houses. After L'Enfant's dismissal as city planner, his vision was never realized, and the Mall remained a swampy area used for markets during the nineteenth century. The Mall was also home to the city's railway station until Union Station opened in 1908.

In 1902, the McMillan Commission set forth to improve the condition of the city's parks. The Mall was transformed into a green space lined by elm trees, and was to be surrounded by museums and scientific organizations only. By 1990, the National Mall was home to nine Smithsonian museums and the two National Galleries of Art. More recently, the National Museum of the American Indian and the World War II Memorial opened in 2004, with the National Martin Luther King Jr. Memorial scheduled to open in 2008.

A City of Protests

The Founding Fathers ensured Americans the rights to assemble and speak freely. In the 20th century especially, Washington, D.C., became the destination for the disenfranchised, the impoverished, the oppressed, and the fearful to gather and voice their opinions to the lawmakers, policy makers, and budget spenders of Washington.

With nearly one-third of the American workforce unemployed and in desperate need of relief during the Great Depression, World War I veterans traveled to Washington seeking early disbursement of their military pension funds. The **Bonus March of 1932** brought approximately 20,000 veterans and their families to Washington. They set up a tent-and-shack encampment, which was called "Hooverville" as a jab at President Hoover. George S. Patton, a cavalry major at the time, was part of the federal force ordered to break up the protest and the camp. Patton considered this assignment his most distasteful form of service to the country.

In 1939, Marian Anderson, the great contralto, was barred from performing at Constitution Hall because she was African-American. The Hall was owned by the Daughters of the American Revolution (DAR). First Lady Eleanor Roosevelt resigned from the DAR in protest and supported the NAACP as it organized an Easter Sunday concert on the grounds of the Lincoln Memorial. More than 75,000 people turned out for the concert, one of the largest crowds to have gathered on the Mall at that time.

THE NATIONAL MALL

On August 28, 1963, the **March on Washington for Jobs and Freedom** came together at the steps of the Lincoln Memorial. Organized by Bayard Rustin and led by union leader A. Philip Randolph, more than 200,000 people participated. Supporters included clergy of all faiths, workers, students, professionals, and celebrities including Sammy Davis Jr., Marlon Brando, Joan Baez, and Bob Dylan. It was here that the Reverend Dr. Martin Luther King Jr. told the world of his dream.

MARCH OF 1932

On November 15, 1969, an estimated 600,000 protesters gathered around the Washington Monument to protest the Vietnam War. Organized by the **New Mobilization Committee to End the War in Vietnam**, the rally was one of the largest in American history and was part of a three-day "Mobilization" to stop the war. Protesters enjoyed music and sang songs advocating peace. The highlight occurred when the audience, led by singer-songwriter-activist Pete Seeger, joined hands and sang John Lennon's recently released anti-war song, "Give Peace a Chance."

After the safety failures at Three Mile Island in March of 1979, a **"No Nukes"** rally drew 100,000 protestors against atomic energy. President Jimmy Carter viewed the mass of humanity from a helicopter and met with activists the next day.

DR. MARTIN LUTHER KING JR. AT THE MARCH ON WASHINGTON FOR JOBS AND FREEDOM

The AIDS Memorial Quilt has been displayed in its entirety only five times—each of which has been on the National Mall. The first display was on October 11, 1987, during the **National March on Washington for Lesbian and Gay Rights**. The quilt—with each panel remembering an individual AIDS victim—covered an area larger than a football field. Sadly, the quilt has grown considerably larger over the years. The last display of the entire AIDS Memorial Quilt was in October 1996, and the quilt covered the eastern expanse of the National Mall. The quilt now features some 44,000 panels, and if it were ever fully displayed again, it would stretch from the U.S. Capitol Building past the Washington Monument to the Lincoln Memorial.

The **Million Man March** was convened by Nation of Islam leader Louis Farrakhan on October 16, 1995. Speakers were critical of the conservative movement of Republicans to the far right after the 1994 congressional elections—characterized as an attack on programs like welfare, Medicaid, housing, student aid, and education. The event included efforts to register African-Americans to vote and to increase black involvement in volunteerism and community activism.

On April 22, 2000, 500,000 people gathered in Washington for **Earth Day 2000** to protest outdated government regulations that did not address global warming. Leonardo DiCaprio was the event chairperson, and Vice President Al Gore gave an impassioned speech as a harbinger to his award-winning documentary *An Inconvenient Truth*.

On May 14, 2000, an estimated Mother's Day holiday crowd of 500,000 gathered for the **Million Mom March** on the National Mall to foster handgun violence awareness. Speakers included Rosie O'Donnell, Susan Sarandon, and Hillary Rodham Clinton, as well as mothers and grandmothers who had lost children to gun violence. Organized after the massacre at Columbine High School in Colorado, where fourteen students and one teacher were killed, the protest called for the passage of stricter handgun laws.

NATIONAL GALLERY OF ART EAST { PAST }

The East Building, or wing, of the National Gallery of Art was designed by the famed I.M. Pei—the master of high modernist architecture—and opened on June 1, 1978, with President Jimmy Carter presiding. Pei's distinguished and diverse designs include the Pyramids of the Louvre in Paris, the Jacob Javits Convention Center in New York City, and the Rock and Roll Hall of Fame in Cleveland, Ohio. It is agreed that the marble monolithic design of the National Gallery of Art East fittingly compliments both the art on display and the design of the west wing of the gallery.

NATIONAL GALLERY OF ART EAST { PRESENT }

The East Building houses modern and contemporary art, with a collection that includes works by Picasso, Matisse, Pollock, Warhol, Lichtenstein, O'Keeffe, and Calder. The East Building also contains the main offices of the National Gallery of Art and a large research facility, the Center for Advanced Study in the Visual Arts. The museum is not technically a part of the Smithsonian Institution, but it is one of the more than ninety cultural institutions in the United States that are Smithsonian "affiliate museums." In 1999, a six-acre sculpture garden was added to the galleries.

NATIONAL GALLERY OF ART WEST { PAST }

Andrew Mellon, financier and art collector, conceived of and funded the creation of this museum. The West Building, or wing, was designed by architect John Russell Pope. It is neoclassical in its design, with a colossal, columned portico and dome—a design that he would later also use for the Jefferson Memorial. The West Building was completed in March 1941 and was, at the time, the largest marble structure in the world.

LORE & LEGEND

The National Gallery of Art West is located on the site where, in 1881, President James Garfield was assassinated by Charles Julius Guiteau.

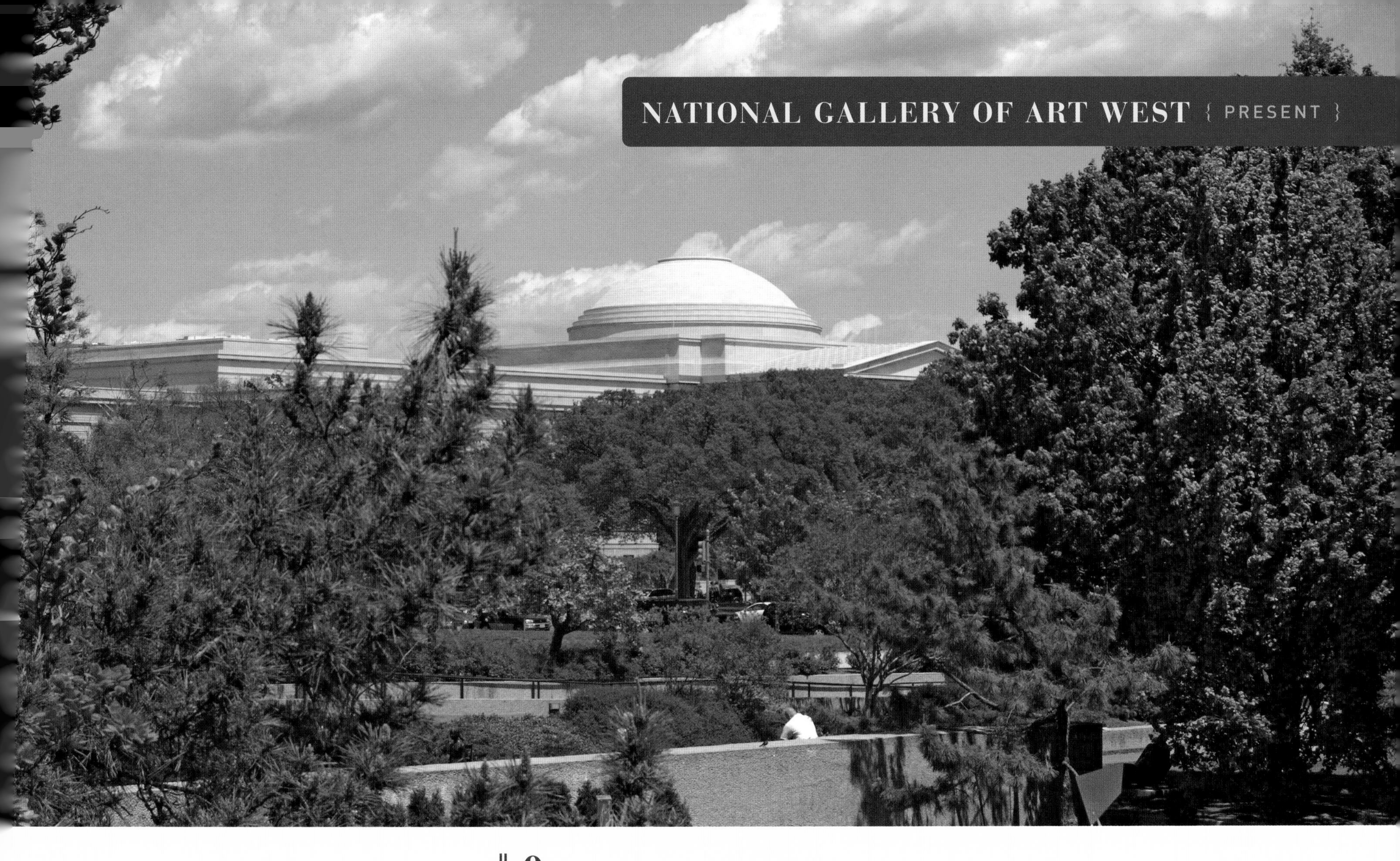

NATIONAL GALLERY OF ART WEST { PRESENT }

Over the years, the National Gallery of Art has come to house one of the finest collections in the world. The West Building contains European paintings and sculpture dating from the 13th century to the 19th century, American art, drawings, decorative arts, and temporary exhibits. The building is so large that the galleries are numbered one to ninety-three and are grouped by chronology and nationality. Highlights of the collection include works by Vermeer, Titian, Rembrandt, Monet, Van Gogh, and da Vinci.

NATIONAL MUSEUM OF NATURAL HISTORY { PAST }

When it first opened in 1910, the United States National Museum—as it was then called—served as home to a wide-ranging collection that included fine art and historical objects in addition to the natural history specimens that are its sole focus today. Designed by Joseph C. Hornblower and J. Rush Marshall, the Beaux Arts–style structure featured a dome of green slate crowning a four-story rotunda. In the early 1960s, wings were added to the east and west sides of the original building, resulting in a museum that today covers about four acres on the Mall.

NATIONAL MUSEUM OF NATURAL HISTORY { PRESENT }

Renamed the National Museum of Natural History in 1968, the facility welcomes more than eight million visitors a year and, since its opening, has become the most visited museum in the world. People arrive from near and far, eager to view the myriad of unique treasures on display—from halls filled with fossilized dinosaur skeletons to galleries filled with rare minerals and gems, including the legendary Hope Diamond.

NATIONAL MUSEUM OF AMERICAN HISTORY { PAST }

This 1972 photograph shows the north facade of the National Museum of History and Technology, which is situated between the Washington Monument and the National Museum of Natural History. From its inception, the museum has displayed an amazing assortment of artifacts including the John Bull steam locomotive, the 1903 Winston touring car that was the first to drive cross-country, Thomas Edison's light bulb from 1879, Samuel Morse's telegraph, Alexander Graham Bell's first telephone, and the flag that inspired Francis Scott Key to write "The Star-Spangled Banner."

NATIONAL MUSEUM OF AMERICAN HISTORY { PRESENT }

Renamed the National Museum of American History in 1980, the museum continues to display information and artifacts on the technological developments of science, industry, transportation, agriculture, and the most important events in the country's history. The collection now totals more than three million pieces. The museum also has a lighter side, with exhibits from the world of entertainment including Mister Rogers' red cardigan, Archie Bunker's recliner, Dorothy's "ruby slippers" from *The Wizard of Oz*, and President Bill Clinton's saxophone.

WASHINGTON MONUMENT { PAST }

Built intermittently between 1848 and 1884, the Washington Monument is the world's tallest masonry structure and arguably the most instantly recognizable monument in the capital city. Standing 555 feet, 5⅛ inches tall, the monument was designed by Robert Mills, who had originally planned a more elaborate structure that included a statue of Washington riding in a chariot. However, lack of funding meant his design had to be scaled back, resulting in the simple stone obelisk that has come to symbolize both the first president and the city that is his namesake.

WASHINGTON MONUMENT { PRESENT }

Today, the Washington Monument presides over the District's landscape in a way that is unrivaled by any other building in the city, thanks to a law prohibiting the construction of buildings taller than the Capitol. Since the monument was already standing when the 1899 law was passed, it became the tallest structure allowed in Washington, D.C. As a result, visitors who take the opportunity to visit the top of the monument are treated to an unobstructed view of the nation's capital.

REFLECTING POOL { PAST }

The Reflecting Pool was designed by Henry Bacon and Charles McKim in 1920. It is a little less than 170 feet wide and close to one-third of a mile long. Its depth is eighteen inches on the sides, sloping to a depth of thirty inches in the center. The pool holds about 6,750,000 gallons of water and reflects the images of the Washington Monument and the Lincoln Memorial. This picture, taken in July 1926, is titled, "Due to the failure of congress to appropriate money for public pools in Washington . . . "

The past practice of swimming in the Reflecting Pool has dwindled greatly due to concerns over the cleanliness of the water, but there are still model boat races in the summer and ice skating in the winter. The Reflecting Pool is one of the city's most popular meeting places as it beckons one to sit and relax by the water or under a shady tree. Beyond the pedestrian paths are other points of interest: To the right of the Reflecting Pool, as one faces the Lincoln Memorial, are the Constitutional Gardens and the Vietnam Veterans and World War II Memorials. To the left side of the pool is the U.S. Marine Corps War Memorial.

WHITE HOUSE { PAST }

In 1814, after the mansion at 1600 Pennsylvania Avenue—home to the U.S. President—was nearly burned to the ground by British troops, the original architect, James Hoban, was called in to oversee rebuilding efforts. When the new building rose from the ashes, a fresh coat of whitewash was applied to the exterior, inspiring the nickname the White House, which would not actually become the official moniker of the president's home until 1901.

The White House has undergone many changes since it first came into use in 1800. The president's office—the Oval Office—was added in 1909, and an entire third floor was built in the 1920s. A second-story porch with an iron railing was added to the South Portico by President Harry Truman, overriding objections of those who felt that the new addition spoiled the look of the mansion. However, the porch proved to be a success and just part of the evolution of the nation's most famous residence.

The White House

A VERY EARLY PHOTO OF THE WHITE HOUSE

The White House. It is a residence, an office, an event-and-banquet facility, a symbol of pride, an important part of and setting for American history. It is, by far, the most famous home in the United States.

As the country's first elected leader, George Washington said, "I walk on untrodden ground. There is scarcely any part of my conduct which may not hereafter be drawn into precedent." One of those precedents was to oversee the design and construction of a suitable home for the president.

Washington understood the importance of presentation, both as a military leader and from his experiences in dealing with European diplomats and royalty. As such, he insisted that the home of the president be made of stone and be of a size and design that symbolized command and dignity. A frugal businessman whose own Mount Vernon manor was made to look like stone by using beveled pine blocks and faux stone paint, Washington had a grand vision and would not compromise. He also believed that, as the first public building in the District, the presidential residence would set a design precedent. As for the interior, Washington favored oval rooms for receiving guests so that all attending could see each other.

George Washington—who called the building the President's House—laid the first cornerstone in 1792. (The sandstone used in its original construction came from the Aquia Creek region of Virginia.) Architect James Hoban's original plans were for a three-story building, but a lack of funds and skilled stonemasons caused slow progress and resulted, after eight years of construction, in a two-story residence. Washington died in 1799, two years after his presidency ended and one year before John Adams came to live in the house that George built.

In a letter to his wife saying the house was ready for her to come and take up residence, Adams wrote, "I pray heaven to bestow the best blessings on this house and all that shall hereafter inhabit it. May none but honest and wise men ever rule under this roof." To his disappointment, he lost his bid for re-election and lived in the house for about four months. Whether Adams would have been further disappointed that his prayers were not answered is a topic debated by seemingly wise and usually honest men to this very day. Regardless of the qualities of its victors, the good house stands as ready now as it did then.

The White House has gone through more than 200 years of expansion and renovation, one catastrophic fire in 1814, and an estimated forty coats of paint. The Oval Office was built in 1909, and a third floor was added to the structure in 1927 when the roof was replaced. The Roosevelts both added

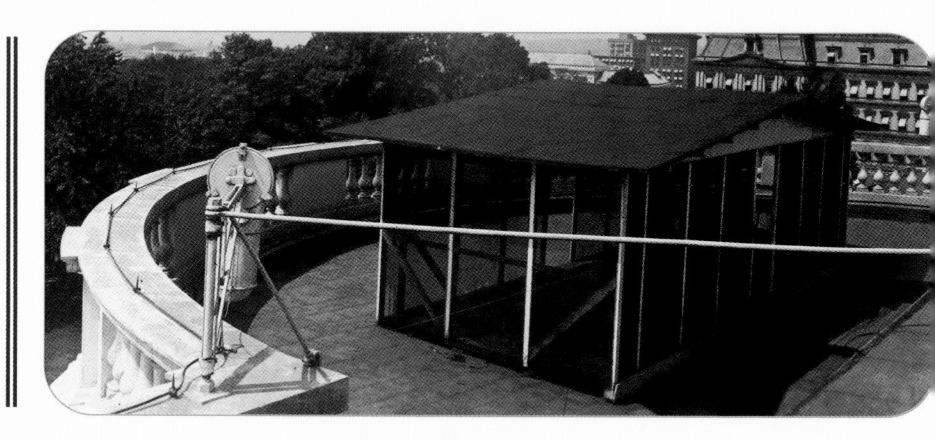

A SLEEPING PORCH ON THE SOUTH PORTICO

wings to the White House: Theodore, the West Wing in 1902; Franklin, the East one about forty years later. President Harry S. Truman added the second floor balcony on the south front of the house.

During the 1830s administration of Andrew Jackson, funds became available for the White House to be fitted with indoor plumbing. James Polk's administration of the 1840s was enlightened by the addition of gas fixtures. In 1892, Benjamin Harrison had electricity installed to supplement the gas. The Harrisons, however, were wary of the modern energy source and refused to operate light switches, leaving them on all night.

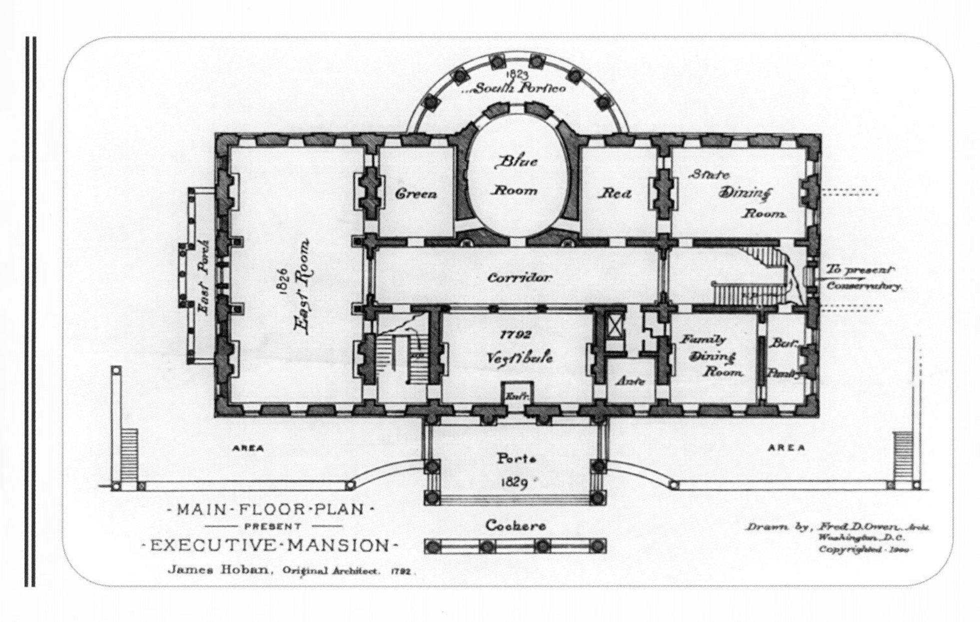

JAMES HOBAN'S ORIGINAL PLANS

In the 1850s, Millard Fillmore updated the kitchen during his time in the White House. He brought in a commercial-use iron stove that the cook could not figure out, sending Fillmore to the Library of Congress to get the instructions.

Today, the White House has an indoor tennis court, jogging track, swimming pool, movie theater, and billiard room. Richard Nixon called himself "an introvert in an extrovert's profession." He had a single-lane bowling alley installed and would bowl late at night, often alone.

THE WHITE HOUSE KITCHEN

President Bill Clinton was in office for the 200th anniversary of John Adams's taking residency of the White House. At the time of its bicentennial, the house had 132 rooms, and the State Dining Room could seat 130 guests.

What about the vice president? Congress secured Number One Observatory Circle from the Navy in 1974 to be used as the vice president's residence. Built in 1893, the Queen Anne–style house lacks offices, meeting rooms, and other general quarters, but it actually has more living space than the White House.

A CURRENT PHOTO OF THE WHITE HOUSE

LAFAYETTE SQUARE { PAST }

Lafayette Square is a seven-acre public park located directly north of the White House on H Street between 15th and 17th Streets, NW. In the earliest plans for the city, this area—the elegant grounds surrounding the executive mansion—was called "President's Park." In 1804, President Thomas Jefferson separated the park from the residence so that Pennsylvania Avenue could cut through. In 1824, the square was officially named in honor of General Lafayette of France. In its early days, the park was home to a racetrack, a graveyard, a zoo, a slave market, and an encampment for soldiers during the War of 1812.

LAFAYETTE SQUARE { PRESENT }

Today, Lafayette Square is home to many political protests and celebrations. In the center of the square is Clark Mill's statue of Andrew Jackson on a rearing horse, erected in 1853. The four corner statues are foreign-born Revolutionary War heroes: France's Marquis de Lafayette and Comte Jean de Rochambeau, Poland's Thaddeus Kosciuszko, and Prussia's Baron Friedrich von Steuben. In 1970, the square and its surrounding structures were designated a National Historic Landmark District.

RENWICK GALLERY { PAST }

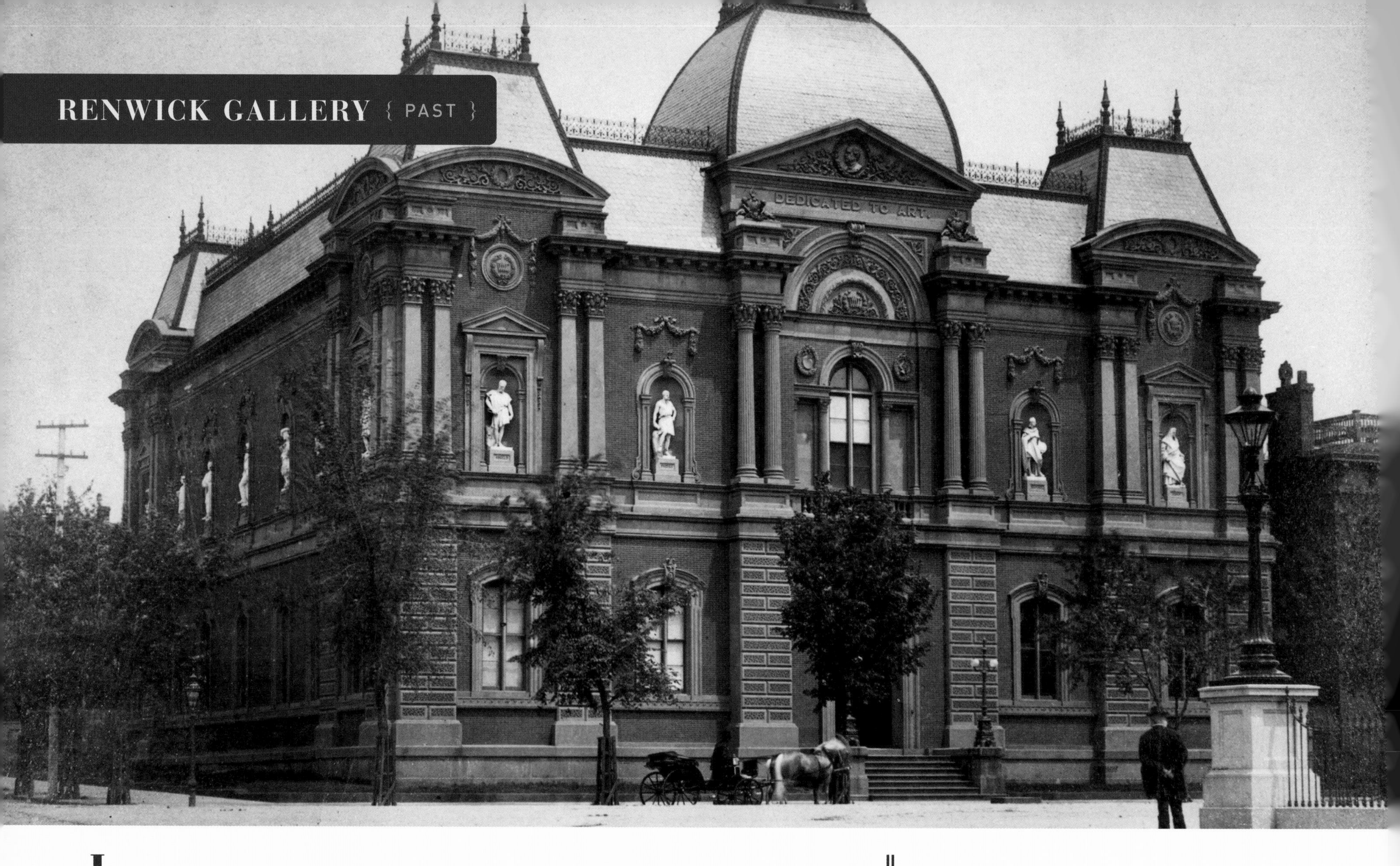

In 1858—after completing the Smithsonian Castle—James Renwick designed this French-influenced Second Empire mansion, which housed the Corcoran Gallery until 1897, when a much larger Corcoran Gallery of Art opened three blocks away. The U.S. Court of Claims used the building from 1899 until 1964, when it was slated for demolition. First Lady Jacqueline Kennedy led the effort to save it and succeeded.

RENWICK GALLERY { PRESENT }

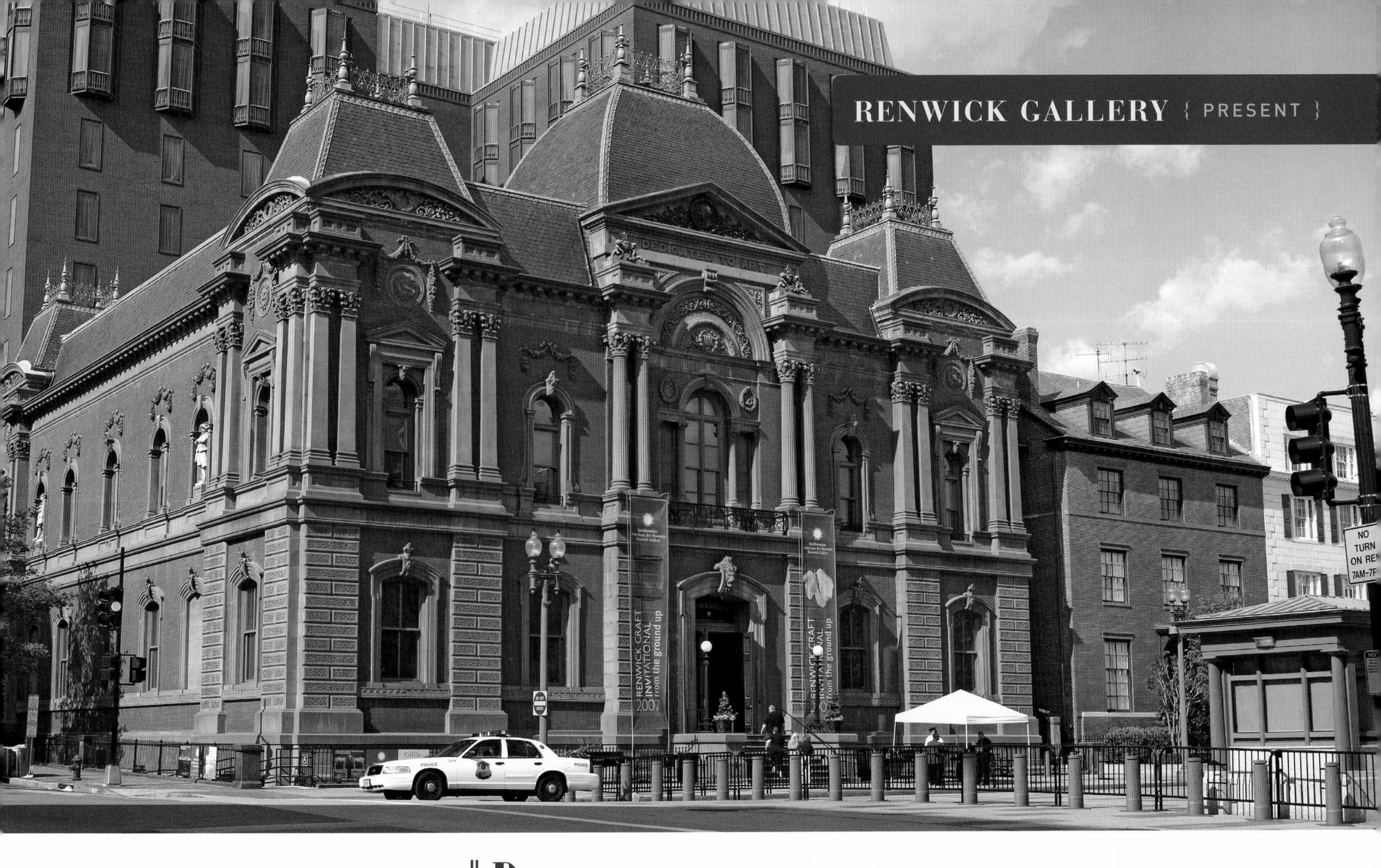

Re-opened in 1972 as the Renwick Gallery in honor of its architect, the museum now houses a portion of the Smithsonian's art, crafts, and design collection. The museum's Grand Salon was restored to its original glory and refurbished in 2000. The space is ninety feet long, with a ceiling soaring forty feet high, and contains masterpieces by John Singer Sargent and Winslow Homer. One can clearly see that many of the statues adorning the building in the early photograph have been replaced by windows. The large building behind the gallery is the New Executive Office Building.

OLD EXECUTIVE OFFICE BUILDING { PAST }

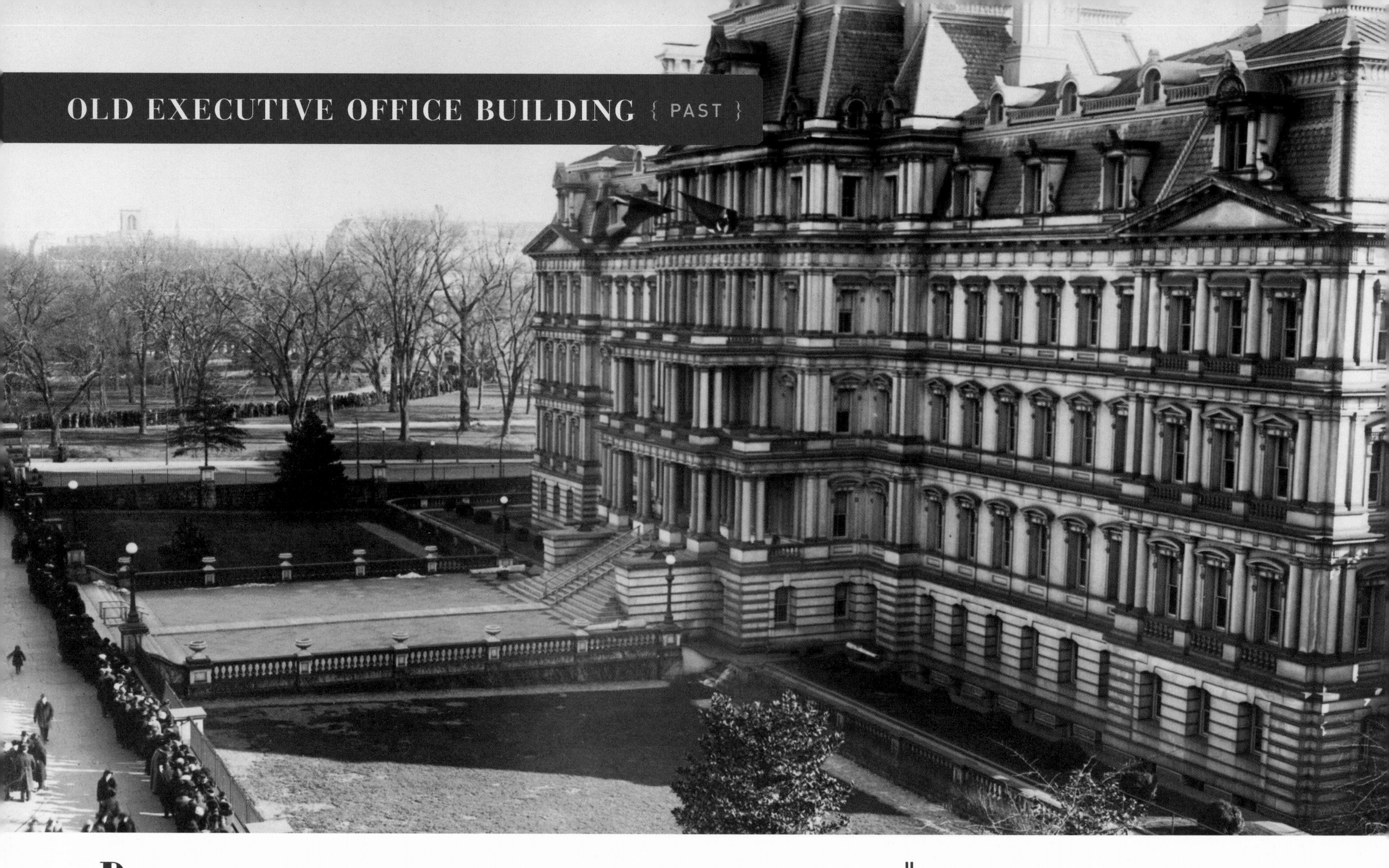

Built between 1871 and 1888, the Old Executive Office Building originally housed the State, War, and Navy departments. Though most of the government buildings erected at this time were given Neoclassical designs, chief architect Alfred Mullett used the same French Second Empire style of architecture of the original Corcoran Gallery (now the Renwick), which stands just across Pennsylvania Avenue. Upon completion, the public did not care for the building's look. Impressive nonetheless, the building has more than 550 rooms and 1,500 windows. This photo from 1922 shows a very long line of people waiting to tour the White House.

OLD EXECUTIVE OFFICE BUILDING { PRESENT }

Public criticism of the outward appearance of the Old Executive Office Building continued, and after its original occupants departed in the 1930s and 1940s, the edifice was left to deteriorate. The Office of the President appropriated it as an annex, and it became known as the Dwight D. Eisenhower Executive Office Building. The Kennedy administration promoted its rehabilitation after years of neglect. Full restoration began in 1983. No longer accessible to the public, the building now houses the National Security Council and the Office of the Vice President.

CORCORAN GALLERY OF ART { PAST }

In 1874, the Corcoran Gallery of Art opened in the building now known as the Renwick Gallery and was the city's first art museum. Named after the banker-philanthropist William Wilson Corcoran, it was founded "for the purpose of encouraging American Genius." The collection grew too large and moved to its present edifice (above) in 1897. Architect Ernest Flagg—designer of the chapel at Annapolis—won the competition to design the new building on its trapezoidal lot. Architect Frank Lloyd Wright called the Beaux Arts–style Corcoran Gallery "the best designed building in Washington."

CORCORAN GALLERY OF ART { PRESENT }

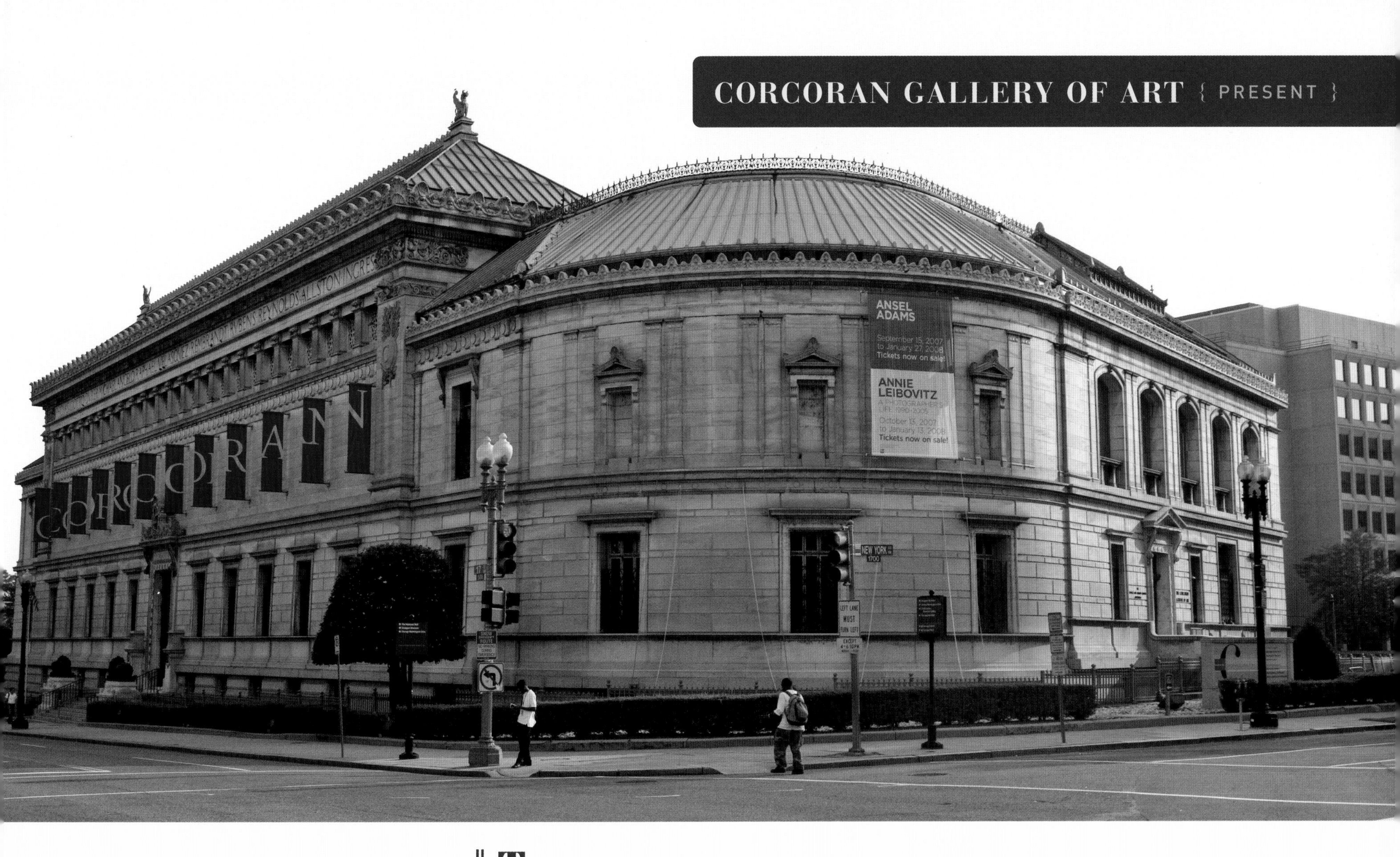

The largest non-federal art museum in the city, the Corcoran is a center for study and a gallery displaying a world-class collection of American, European, and contemporary art. Two of its most important pieces are *Washington Before Yorktown* by Rembrandt Peale and *Niagara* by Frederic Church. Attendance continued to grow at a rapid pace through the 1990s, and a new wing, designed by Frank O. Gehry, was to be added. The expansion plan stalled in 2005, however, when private funding fell short.

VIETNAM VETERANS MEMORIAL { PAST }

The Vietnam Veterans Memorial—or "The Wall," as it is popularly known—is the brainchild of Vietnam veteran Jan Scruggs. Concerned that the service and sacrifice of men and women who fought in the controversial war would be forgotten, Scruggs founded the Vietnam Veterans Memorial Foundation. After an initially slow start, donations began to pour in, and the federal government donated two acres of land between the Washington Monument and the Lincoln Memorial to serve as the location of a new memorial.

VIETNAM VETERANS MEMORIAL { PRESENT }

A competition was held to select a design for the memorial, and more than 1,400 entries were submitted. The winning design, the work of a young college student named Maya Lin, was an austere black wall carved with the names of the more than 58,000 Americans who died in the Vietnam War. Although there was some early resistance to the design, most opposition vanished during the dedication in 1983 when it became obvious that the public responded to the simplicity and accessibility of the new memorial.

LINCOLN MEMORIAL { PAST }

In 1914, construction of the Lincoln Memorial began on a hillock of marshland reclaimed from the Potomac River. The architect, Henry Bacon, drew his inspiration for the neoclassical building from a mixture of Greek and Roman elements. At the heart of the memorial is a nineteen-foot-tall statue of a seated Abraham Lincoln, designed by Daniel Chester French, who worked from photographs and a life mask of the sixteenth president.

LINCOLN MEMORIAL { PRESENT }

In the years since its dedication in 1922, the Lincoln Memorial has become a symbol of American democracy and the Civil Rights movement. In 1939, when African-American contralto Marian Anderson was denied the opportunity to sing at Constitution Hall, First Lady Eleanor Roosevelt invited her to appear at the Lincoln Memorial. The memorial was later the site of Martin Luther King Jr.'s "I Have a Dream" speech in 1963, one of the defining moments in the Civil Rights movement and American history.

JOHN F. KENNEDY CENTER FOR THE PERFORMING ARTS { PAST }

President Dwight D. Eisenhower first signed legislation to build a national performance venue in 1958, but a lack of private funding delayed construction. Once the building was renamed for President Kennedy and given the designation of being a living memorial to him, interest and donations increased. In 1971, the John F. Kennedy Center for the Performing Arts opened on the shores of the Potomac as one of the nation's premiere cultural centers. The building offered the community an opera house, several theaters, and a concert hall, all in one impressive facility. The building is clad in white Carrara marble, a gift from Italy.

JOHN F. KENNEDY CENTER FOR THE PERFORMING ARTS { PRESENT }

There are two entrances to the Kennedy Center. The north entrance, called the Hall of States, displays flags from all fifty states. The south entrance, called the Hall of Nations, displays flags from all the countries that are diplomatically affiliated with the United States. The grand foyer is 630 feet long and lit by eighteen chandeliers, gifts from Sweden. The foyer's walls have nine fifty-eight-foot-tall mirrors that were donated by Belgium. The Kennedy Center is home to the world-renowned National Symphony Orchestra.

WATERGATE { PAST }

In 1960, the Italian real estate company Societa Generale Immobiliare purchased a triangular parcel of land from the Washington Gas and Light Company with the intention of developing the ten acres into a complex of mixed-use buildings. Luigi Moretti, the renowned Italian Modernist, was chief architect. After overcoming initial opposition to the size and heights of the proposed buildings, construction began in 1964 and was completed in 1971. A certain bungled burglary attempt in the early hours of June 17, 1972, secured Watergate's place as a significant building in American history.

The name Watergate is still remembered as the setting where "plumbers" broke into the Democratic National Committee headquarters, setting off the notorious sequence of events that led to President Richard Nixon's resignation in August of 1974. Various buildings in the complex—which includes a hotel, two office buildings, three apartment buildings, and a retail center—have changed hands through the years. Watergate VIP residents have included Bob and Elizabeth Dole, U.S. Supreme Court Justice Ruth Bader Ginsberg, and Condoleezza Rice. The complex was added to the National Register of Historic Places in 2005.

U. S. MARINE CORPS WAR MEMORIAL { PAST }

Sandwiched between the epic conflict that was World War II and the harrowing divisiveness of the Vietnam War, the Korean War has often been called the "Forgotten War." In 1984, Hal Barker, the son of a Korean War veteran, helped establish the Korean War Memorial Trust Fund with the aim of commemorating the heroic sacrifices of the men and women who fought in that war. Construction of the memorial began in 1986, ending with President Bill Clinton and South Korean President Kim Young Sam taking part in the memorial's dedication ceremony in 1995.

U. S. MARINE CORPS WAR MEMORIAL { PRESENT }

"Freedom is not free." This simple truth, inscribed on a wall at the Korean War Veterans Memorial, reminds visitors that liberty sometimes comes at a high price. The memorial includes several features: a black granite wall etched with the faces of American servicemen, a granite curb listing the twenty-two countries that provided troops or support during the conflict, and a group of nineteen sculpted figures spread out as if marching across a field, representing American soldiers on patrol. A nearby Pool of Remembrance provides a quiet place for visitors to pause and reflect.

TIDAL BASIN { PAST }

The Tidal Basin connects the Potomac River to the Washington Channel. The tranquil body of water was once a natural swampy inlet that was developed in the 1880s for aesthetic and functional reasons. It is about ten feet deep and covers a little more than one hundred acres. Its water level is maintained by an inlet gate at the Potomac and an outflow into the Washington Channel. Twice daily with the changing tide, water, silt, and sediment flow through the channel and into the Anacostia River to the south. The photo above was taken in the 1920s.

As one can see from this recent photograph, additional sidewalks and fences have been added along the Tidal Basin, making fishing more challenging than in the past. The large body of water complements its surroundings by allowing long views to show off the famed cherry trees that nearly encircle the basin and enhance the majestic stance of the Jefferson Memorial. Though swimming in the basin was banned in 1925, pedal boats traverse it during the warmer months.

CHERRY BLOSSOMS { PAST }

The first gift of cherry blossom trees, called *sakura* in Japanese, was delivered to Washington in 1909. Unfortunately, the trees had to be destroyed because they were infested by insects and disease. Three years later, Tokyo mayor Yukio Ozaki sent a healthy batch. On March 27, 1912, First Lady Helen Taft and the wife of the Japanese ambassador, Viscountess Chinda, planted the first two cherry blossom trees in West Potomac Park. In 1915, the United States sent a gift of flowering dogwood trees to Japan. Over the next seven years, several thousand cherry trees were planted around the Tidal Basin.

CHERRY BLOSSOMS { PRESENT }

In 1958, the Japanese government presented Washington with a stone pagoda and a 17th-century granite lantern to commemorate Commodore Perry's voyage to Japan in the 1850s. Both gifts now sit among the trees on the west bank of the Tidal Basin. In 1982, Japanese horticulturists came to collect cuttings that will be used to replace trees lost in future flooding. Today, more than 3,700 cherry trees grow around the Tidal Basin, at East Potomac Park, and on the grounds of the Washington Monument.

VIEWING THE BLOSSOMS BY BOAT—PAST

VIEWING THE BLOSSOMS BY BOAT—PRESENT

The National Cherry Blossom Festival

Although the National Cherry Blossom Festival is now an annual event for Washington that draws visitors from around the globe, the first official commemoration of Japan's cherry blossom tree donation did not occur until fifteen years after the planting, when a group of the city's schoolchildren performed a re-enactment of the planting in 1927. The first true festival was held in 1935 and was sponsored by local civic groups, laying the groundwork for the event that is still celebrated today.

Over the years, the Cherry Blossom Festival continued to grow, eventually becoming a popular ritual of spring. In the 1940s, a Cherry Blossom Pageant was introduced, and by 1985, the festival had grown so large that a not-for-profit organization called National Cherry Blossom Festival, Inc., was created to coordinate the event and promote participation. Members are volunteers who represent Washington's civic, government, and business communities and who coordinate the festival, organize seminars, prepare exhibits, and conduct other activities to educate the public about Japanese culture.

months for a team of eight to ten people to complete the task.

Once the buds begin to expand in late February or early March, they are monitored. The days before they can be expected to bloom are counted down on the Web site of the National Park Service. Their best estimate is based upon weather forecasts and close inspection of the trees themselves to determine the stage of bud development.

The two-week festival is kicked off with an opening ceremony, followed by a variety of activities and cultural events. Each day, there are classes about cherry blossoms, a sushi/sake celebration, and bike tours of the Tidal Basin. There are exhibits of photography, sculpture, and animation and various cultural performances throughout Washington, D.C. *Rakugo* (Japanese comedy) performances, kimono fashion shows, dancing, singing, martial arts, and much more can also be seen.

The Cherry Blossom Ten-Mile Run is held as part of the festival on the first Sunday in April. On the last Saturday, there is the Parade of the National Cherry Blossom Festival, followed by the Sakura Matsuri-Japanese Street Festival, a celebration presented by the Japan–America Society of Washington, D.C. More than 750,000 people visit Washington each year to admire the blossoming cherry trees that herald the beginning of spring in the nation's capital.

STROLLING BENEATH THE BLOSSOMS

In 1994, the festival was expanded to two weeks) accommodate a greater variety of activities lanned around the tree-blooming celebration.

Maintenance of a cherry blossom tree, like ny other plant, requires watering, fertilization, nd pruning. Caring for the 3,700 trees is crucial when a two-week festival is held in their honor every year. The average life span of the trees is fifty to sixty years, but they can live up to one hundred if given fairly intensive care. The largest threat posed to the blossoms is a late frost, which could cause a bloomless festival but not hurt the trees themselves. The National Park Service prunes the trees twice yearly. It takes three

JEFFERSON MEMORIAL { PAST }

In 1934, President Franklin D. Roosevelt appointed a commission to correct what he felt was a glaring deficiency in Washington, D.C.: the lack of a monument to Thomas Jefferson, a Founding Father and president whose ideals and values had been instrumental in the founding of the United States. John Russell Pope, one of the country's foremost architects, was assigned the task of designing a suitable structure and chose as his inspiration the Pantheon in Rome. Roosevelt dedicated the completed monument on April 13, 1943, the 200th anniversary of Jefferson's birth.

JEFFERSON MEMORIAL { PRESENT }

The interior of the memorial features a majestic bronze statue of Jefferson—actually installed four years after the memorial's dedication—and quotations from Jefferson's written works carved into the marble walls. The north entrance to the memorial looks out over the Tidal Basin, which in the spring is ringed by the city's beloved cherry trees, and offers a spectacular view of the Washington Monument and National Mall. The pediment over the north entrance depicts Jefferson's key role in drafting the Declaration of Independence.

SMITHSONIAN CASTLE { PAST }

Designed by James Renwick and completed in 1855, this red sandstone Gothic Revival "castle" was the first building for what today is known the world over as the Smithsonian Institution. When British chemist James Smithson died in 1829, he bequeathed his entire estate—worth nearly half a million dollars—to the United States, a country he had never even visited. His will directed that the money should be used to create " . . . an establishment for the increase and diffusion of knowledge among men."

SMITHSONIAN CASTLE { PRESENT }

After considerable debate, Congress authorized the founding of the Smithsonian Institution in 1846, laying the groundwork for an organization that would eventually become one of the world's greatest museum and research facilities. Today, the Smithsonian is the world's largest museum complex, which includes more than a dozen museums, the National Zoological Park, and a wide variety of research and exploration facilities. The Smithsonian Castle building, no longer a museum, serves as an information center for the millions who visit the complex each year.

SMITHSONIAN ARTS AND INDUSTRIES BUILDING { PAST }

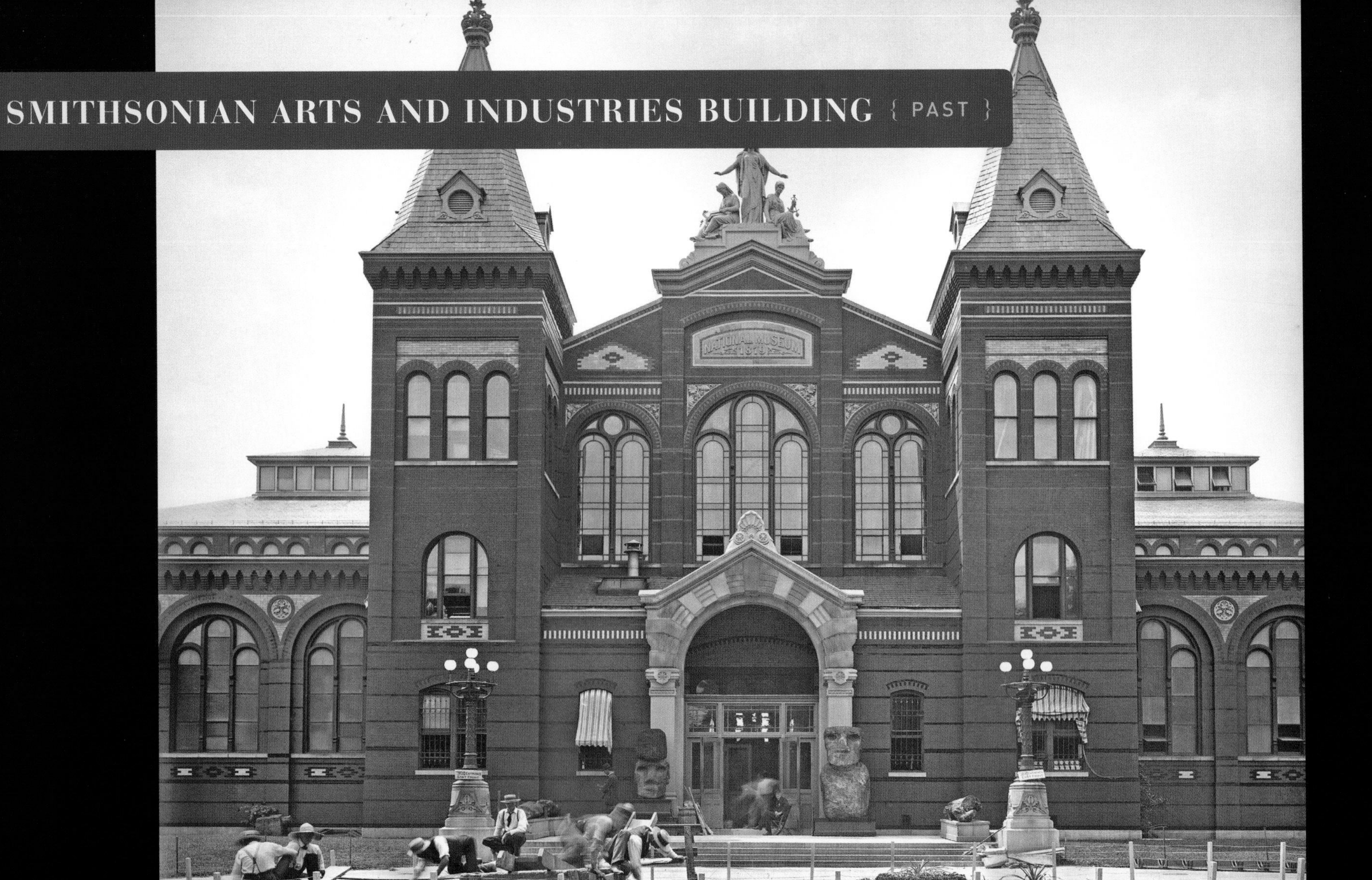

Built next to the Smithsonian Castle, the Arts and Industries Building was completed in 1881, just in time to host President James Garfield's Inaugural Ball. Constructed of brick and red Ohio sandstone and designed in a Victorian Romanesque style, the structure was intended to serve as the National Museum and a new home for the collection featured in the 1876 Philadelphia Centennial Exhibition.

SMITHSONIAN ARTS AND INDUSTRIES BUILDING { PRESENT }

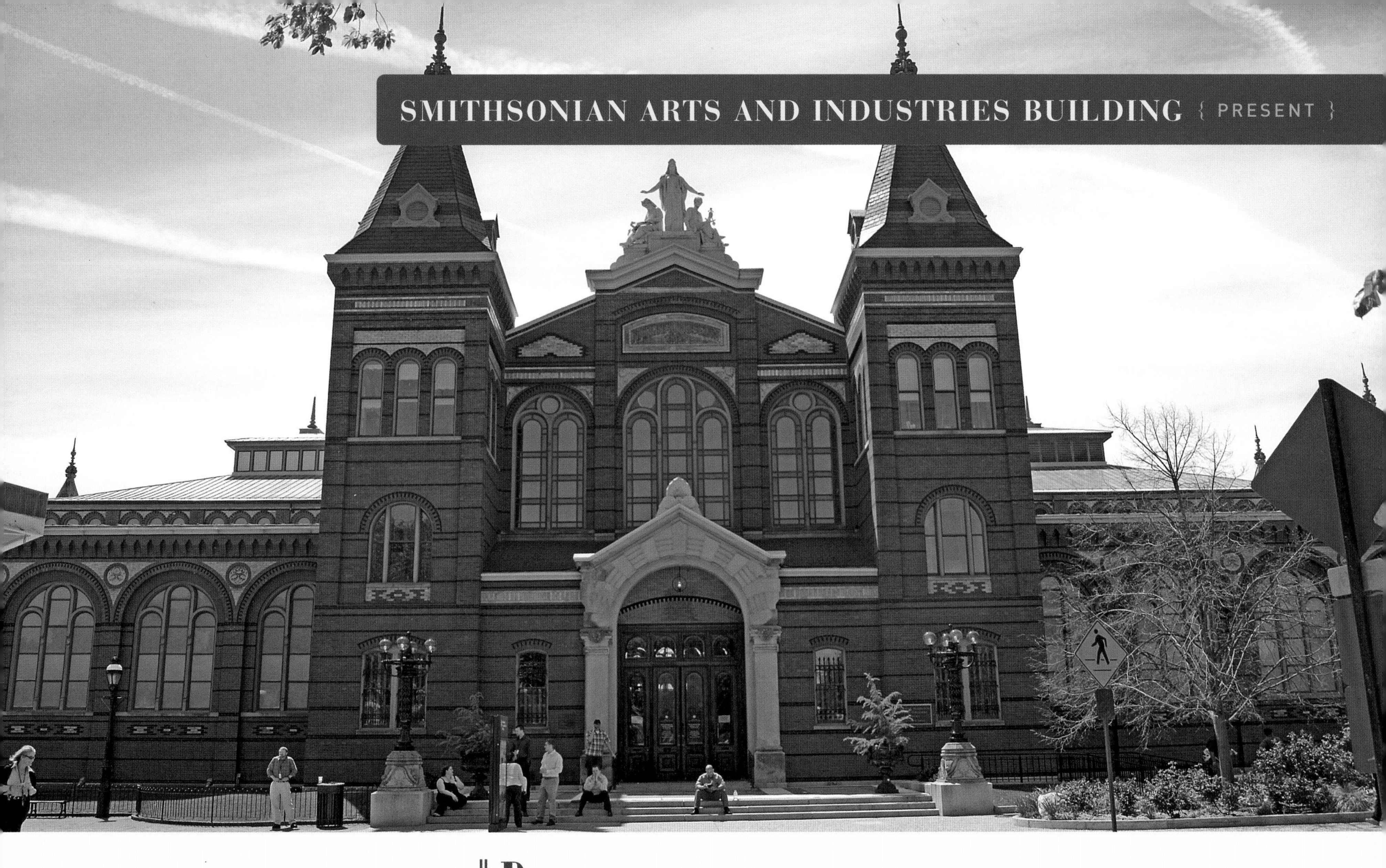

During its first one hundred years, the Arts and Industries Building exhibited nearly all of the Smithsonian's collections—on subjects ranging from natural to American to aviation history. The building was officially designated a National Historical Landmark in 1977. Since then, it has reverted to its original purpose, exhibiting rotating displays of the objects from the 1876 Philadelphia Centennial Exhibition. In addition to the exhibits, the building houses Smithsonian administrative offices.

HIRSHHORN MUSEUM AND SCULPTURE GARDEN { PAST }

Designed by architect Gordon Bunshaft to resemble "a large piece of functional sculpture," the Smithsonian's Hirshhorn Museum and Sculpture Garden is home to one of the world's most important collections of modern and contemporary art. Shaped like a hollow-centered cylinder, the museum building sits atop four enormous concrete piers and surrounds an open courtyard with a fountain. The Sculpture Garden—featuring works by Rodin, Hepworth, and Maillol—is located across Jefferson Drive on the grounds of the National Mall.

HIRSHHORN MUSEUM AND SCULPTURE GARDEN { PRESENT }

Since opening to the public in 1974, the Hirshhorn has steadily built upon the collection of its benefactor and namesake, financier Joseph Hirshhorn. Today, the museum's collection numbers more than 11,500 works by artists ranging from Cassatt and Eakins to Calder and Diebenkorn. The plaza beneath the main building was redesigned in the early 1990s to provide more garden space for visitors to relax and take in the large-scale outdoor sculpture for which the Hirshhorn is renowned.

NATIONAL AIR AND SPACE MUSEUM { PAST }

Congress passed an act in 1946 that called for the creation of a National Air Museum. For years, the large collection was displayed in several different locations, including the Arts and Industries Building and a building in the South Yard of the Smithsonian that was eventually named the Air and Space Building, pictured here. During the Space Race with the Soviet Union, the museum was renamed the National Air and Space Museum, and a new building to house the entire collection was opened in 1976, in time for the country's bicentennial celebration.

NATIONAL AIR AND SPACE MUSEUM { PRESENT }

LORE & LEGEND

In June 1995, after months of controversy over the wording and tone of the information presented, the *Enola Gay* exhibition opened, featuring the restored forward fuselage of the B-29 Superfortress bomber that carried out the mission of dropping an atomic bomb on Hiroshima, Japan, on August 6, 1945.

The museum hosts around ten million visitors annually, and in 2003, a companion facility near Washington Dulles International Airport was opened to provide showrooms for exhibits too large to fit on the National Mall. On display in the two buildings are the Wright brothers' flyer, Lindbergh's *Spirit of St. Louis*, the Space Shuttle *Enterprise*, the B-29 *Enola Gay*, a Lockheed SR-71 Blackbird, an Air France Concorde, the *Apollo 11* command module, and many other aircraft.

REDERICK DOUGLASS HOUSE { PAST }

Built in 1854 by John Van Nook, the house that would come to be known as Cedar Hill was part of a planned residential community, called Uniontown, that never quite caught on with the public. After the Civil War, Frederick Douglass took a position as U.S. Marshall for the District of Columbia and bought the nine-acre estate in 1877. In time, he expanded the property to fifteen acres and enlarged the white brick house, which he named Cedar Hill, to twenty-one rooms.

FREDERICK DOUGLASS HOUSE { PRESENT }

Abolitionist, author, slave, freedman, and adviser to four presidents, Frederick Douglass died at Cedar Hill in 1895 at the age of 77. After her husband's death, Douglass' widow organized a memorial association in her husband's name to preserve the home. After Hurricane Hazel destroyed all but two of the estate's outbuildings in 1967, the house was restored and opened to the public in 1972. Cedar Hill still contains almost all of the original furnishings from Douglass' life.

UNION STATION { PAST }

Faced in white Vermont granite, the Beaux Arts–style station was designed by architect Daniel Burnham and is monumental in every aspect. A testament to the unbounded optimism of the new century, Union Station was completed in 1908 at a then-staggering construction cost of more than $125 million. At the time it was built, the station covered more ground than any other building in the United States and was the largest train station in the world. The Romanesque interior was so impressive that Presidents Taft, Wilson, and Franklin D. Roosevelt received foreign diplomats there.

LORE & LEGEND

Times sure have changed. In its early days, Union Station was home to a mortuary, bowling alley, ice house, and Turkish baths.

UNION STATION { PRESENT }

With the advent of air travel, Union Station fell into decline in the 1950s and 1960s, closing in 1981. After three years of renovation costing $160 million, the city's only railroad station reopened on September 29, 1988. Now a vibrant retail center with more than 130 shops—including a bookstore, boutiques, restaurants, and a movie theater—the station has approximately 70,000 people pass through it daily. Business travelers, military personnel, and savvy locals will wait in long lines for what they claim is the best shoe shine anywhere.

OLD POST { PAST }

Built in 1899 and standing twelve stories tall, the steel-and-granite Old Post building was Washington's first skyscraper and the first government building to have its own power plant. Described as hideous and old-fashioned, the Richardsonian Romanesque building was nicknamed "Old Tooth," and the public and politicians wanted it razed. In 1914, the mail processing division moved to a larger building next to Union Station, and at only fifteen years old, the building was dubbed the "old" post office. After the postmaster left for other offices in 1934, the building quickly deteriorated.

OLD POST { PRESENT }

Through both World Wars, the Great Depression, and many administration changes, the Old Post served as overflow office space for government agencies. The building underwent a $30 million renovation in the 1970s and is now a spacious pavilion with shops, government and private offices, and a food court. The clock tower houses the Congressional Bells, a bicentennial gift from Great Britain. Modeled after those at Westminster Abbey, the ten bells are rung to mark congressional sessions. The view from the top of the tower is one of the best in the city.

FORD'S THEATRE { PAST }

John T. Ford leased a vacant Baptist church on this site in 1861 and converted the building into a music hall called Ford's Atheneum. Fire destroyed the old hall on New Year's Eve 1862, forcing Ford to quickly build his famous 699-seat venue, which opened in August 1863. Though the brick facade was austere in design, the interior was lavishly decorated and was soon acknowledged as one of the finest theaters in the country. On April 14, 1865, only five days after Lee surrendered to Grant at Appomattox, President Abraham Lincoln was assassinated at Ford's Theatre while attending a benefit performance.

LORE & LEGEND

Lincoln attended eight performances at Ford's Theatre during the Civil War—including one play starring his assassin, John Wilkes Booth.

FORD'S THEATRE { PRESENT }

Serving as a living tribute to Lincoln's love of the performing arts, Ford's Theatre reopened in 1968 as a working playhouse and museum. Maintained by the National Park Service, the theater was restored to its original glory of 1865 and now hosts contemporary American plays and musicals. The presidential box eerily appears just as it did on the night of the assassination. The museum contains articles of clothing worn by Lincoln, including a custom-made Brooks Brothers black overcoat, and John Wilkes Booth's .44-caliber derringer, hunting knife, and diary.

A City of Ghosts

If you are susceptible to psychic vibrations from the great beyond, then Washington, D.C., is the place to go to get an otherworldly lesson in American history. Some of the capital's most familiar landmarks are reportedly inhabited by ghosts. With so many strong-willed and determined individuals making up the city's storied past, their "spirits" seem to have refused to move on from this earthly realm. Here is just a sampling of the famous and infamous dead and where they haunt.

Some call it stage fright, while others call it getting spooked. The ghost of actor and Confederate sympathizer **John Wilkes Booth**, the man who assassinated President Abraham Lincoln, is believed to occupy **Ford's Theater**. His ghostly form has been seen by theater employees, audience members, and actors alike. The ghost is allegedly responsible for inexplicable cold spots throughout the theater and for making actors forget their lines. Others claim to see Lincoln's ghost here, as well.

Is it any wonder the **Old Post** has a ghost when the postmaster fell to his death at the building's opening ceremony? According to author John Alexander, the building has had problems with the

FORD'S THEATER

JOHN WILKES BOOTH

elevators, such as doors opening between floors and alarms going off in empty cars. Maybe visitors should take the stairs!

In a bit of parade unrest, the spirit of the Marine Corps 1st Commandant Captain Samuel

WHITE HOUSE LINCOLN BEDROOM

MARINE CORPS BARRACKS ON 8TH STREET SE

Nicholas returns to his former home, the **Marine Corps Barracks** on 8th Street SE. It must be all those Department of Defense forms in triplicate keeping him busy as papers rustling and pacing can be heard in the empty rooms.

ABRAHAM LINCOLN

Although the ghosts of former Presidents **Thomas Jefferson** and **Andrew Jackson**, along with former First Lady **Abigail Adams**, are frequently mentioned as spirit dwellers of the **White House**, the ghost of President **Abraham Lincoln** is reportedly the most active, walking the halls and knocking upon the door to his former bedroom. Lincoln's ghost has not only been seen by White House staffers and residents, but also by heads of state such as Winston Churchill and Queen Wilhelmina of the Netherlands. In fact, Queen Wilhelmina—a White House guest of Franklin D. Roosevelt—was so traumatized by the somber countenance of the murdered president that she fainted straight away.

INDONESIAN EMBASSY

EVALYN WALSH MCLEAN

The **Indonesian Embassy** on Massachusetts Avenue is inhabited by an unlucky—and naked—ghost. **Evalyn Walsh McLean**, the mining heiress, socialite, and last private owner of the supposedly cursed Hope Diamond, led an unhappy life until her death in 1947. Witnesses claim her nude spirit descends the staircase of her former mansion.

Naturally, the oldest house in Washington should have its fair share of residual spectral energies. The **Old Stone House** on M Street in Georgetown is said to have a hostile male ghost and several other apparitions haunting the site.

The **Hay-Adams Hotel**, an elegant and dignified structure in Lafayette Square, was built over the site of the Slidell House where Marian "Clover" Hooper Adams committed suicide. Married to Henry Adams, the grandson of President John Quincy Adams, Clover was subject to bouts of melancholy and took poison to end her life. Her spirit wanders the halls of the hotel with the scent of mimosa trailing behind her.

HAY-ADAMS HOTEL

PETERSEN HOUSE { PAST }

The unassuming Greek revival residence on 10th Street across from Ford's Theater is where President Abraham Lincoln passed away. The physicians attending the fatally wounded president had him carried to this boarding house to avoid the mob gathering in the street, setting guards at the front steps. Once word of the shooting spread through the city, a procession of dignitaries and statesmen came to pay their respects to the country's sixteenth president. Lincoln never regained consciousness and died at 7:22 the morning after he was shot.

PETERSEN HOUSE { PRESENT }

The government bought the house for $30,000 in 1896 but did not reopen it until 1932. Presently, the restored home of William Petersen has been called one of the city's most modest museums, with just three first-floor rooms open to the public. Decorated in Victorian period furnishings, the front parlor is where Mary Todd Lincoln and her son, Robert Todd, held their vigil. Because of his great height, the president was placed diagonally on the small bed. On display is Lincoln's bloodstained pillowcase.

OLD PATENT OFFICE BUILDING { PAST }

Covering an entire city block—bordered by F, G, 7th, and 9th Streets—the Old Patent Office was built between 1836 and 1867. It was only the third federal building constructed in the early years of the city, after the White House and the Capitol, and is one of the finest examples of Greek Revival architecture in the country. The building was a celebration of America's inventiveness and creativity, with wide halls proudly displaying patent models. In 1932, the Patent Office moved to a new location, and other government agencies took occupancy of the building.

LORE & LEGEND

Clara Barton, a clerk in the patent office with little medical training, tended wounded soldiers in these same wide halls during the Civil War. Barton later founded the American Red Cross and is acknowledged as a great humanitarian.

OLD PATENT OFFICE BUILDING { PRESENT }

In 1953, the magnificent building was slated for demolition to make room for a parking lot. The emerging historical preservation movement, thankfully, rescued it. President Dwight D. Eisenhower signed protection legislation and passed stewardship of the building to the Smithsonian. In 1968, the building became the National Portrait Gallery and the National Museum of American Art Museum until January 2000. Private donations totaling tens of millions of dollars were given to the Smithsonian Institution for extensive renovation, and in July 2006, the newly named Smithsonian American Art Museum and the National Portrait Gallery re-opened in a gloriously restored edifice.

HOWARD UNIVERSITY { PAST }

Howard—one of the country's first black universities—was chartered by Congress in 1867. The school was named—against his wishes—in honor of General Oliver O. Howard, who came to Washington after the Civil War and became commissioner of the Bureau of Refugees, Freedmen and Abandoned Lands. Commonly referred to as the Freedmen's Bureau, it sold land to black families and funded education programs for freed people. Under the stewardship of Dr. Mordecai Wyatt Johnson, who served as the school's first black president from 1926 to 1950, Howard University, pictured here in 1942, truly established itself as a preeminent learning center.

HOWARD UNIVERSITY { PRESENT }

LORE & LEGEND

Notable graduates of Howard University include Zora Neale Thurston, Toni Morrison, Vernon Jordan, Ossie Davis, David Dinkins, and Roberta Flack. U.S. Supreme Court Justice Thurgood Marshall attended Howard's law school.

With an enrollment of more than 10,000 students, Howard University is now the country's leading black university and produces more African-American PhDs than any other university in the world. Howard offers academic programs in more than 120 areas of study, in which students can earn undergraduate, graduate, and professional degrees. Between 1998 and 2007, the university produced two Rhodes Scholars, a Truman Scholar, a Marshall Scholar, thirteen Fulbright Scholars, and nine Pickering Fellows.

ADAMS MORGAN { PAST }

Adams Morgan gets its name from two formerly segregated schools in the city's Northwest section: the all-black Thomas P. Morgan Elementary School and the all-white John Quincy Adams Elementary School. In 1954, the Supreme Court ruled that all District of Columbia schools would be desegregated the following year. When the city drew new boundaries to follow the law, the new zone took the name of the schools. This November 1949 photograph is of the Morgan School at the corner of Champlain Street and Florida Avenue NW.

ADAMS MORGAN { PRESENT }

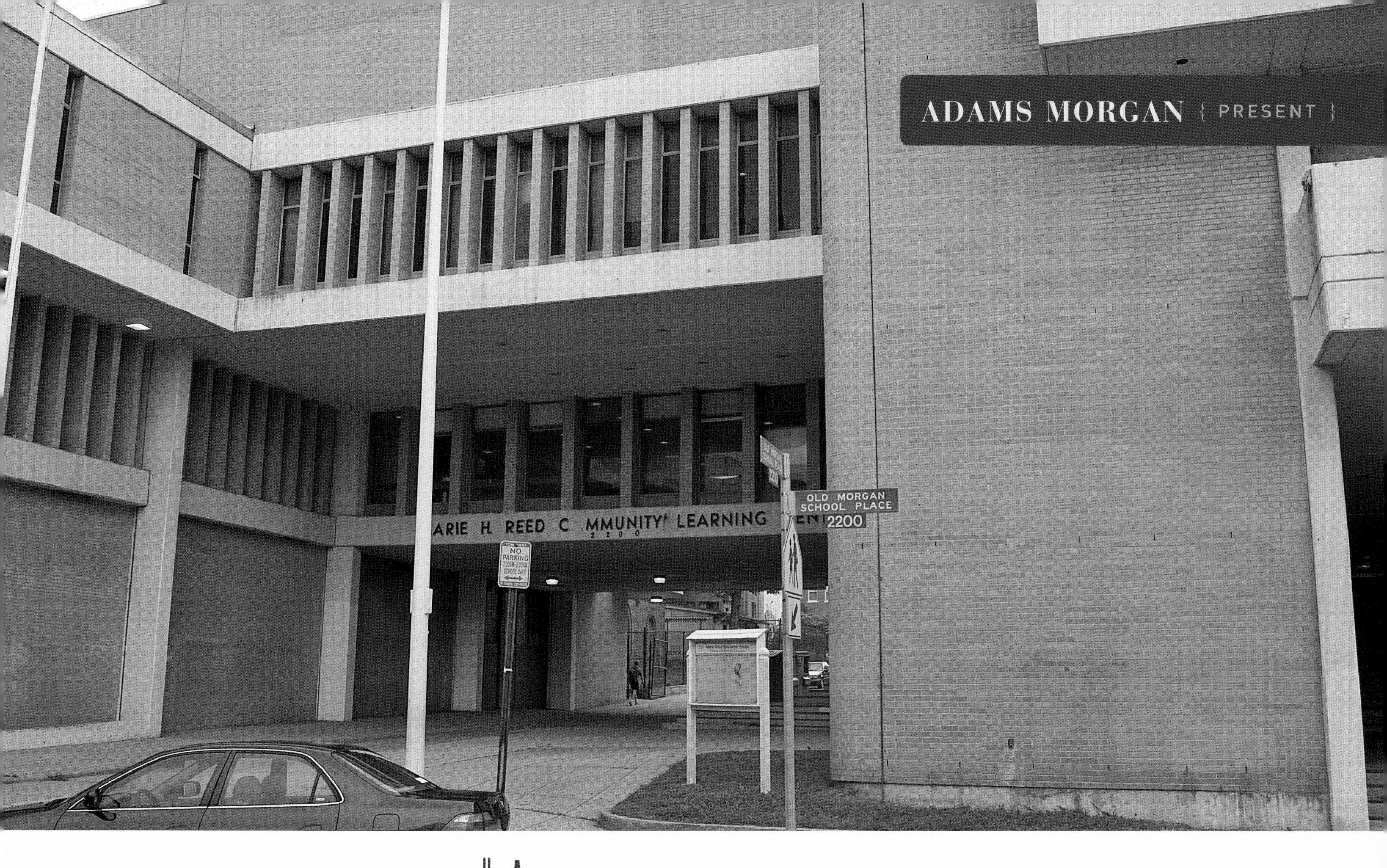

Adams Morgan is known for its cultural diversity and is home, largely, to the city's Latino community. The Morgan School is no longer standing. In the late 1960s, the Marie H. Reed Community Learning Center—a new elementary school and recreational complex that serves as a community hub—was built. The area around U Street suffered after the riots that followed the 1968 assasination of Martin Luther King Jr., but artists and young professionals were lured back in the 1980s and 1990s. Now, Adams Morgan is one of the hippest neighborhoods in the city. *National Geographic* describes the area as "an enclave of bohemian flair in the center of staid Washington."

CONNECTICUT AVENUE { PAST }

Connecticut Avenue, one of the roads in the city's original plans, has long been a major thoroughfare in the District of Columbia. It begins near the White House at the northwest corner of Lafayette Square and runs north through Dupont Circle and past the National Zoo before reaching Chevy Chase, Maryland. The bronze equestrian statue in the photograph is of Army of the Potomac General George B. McClellan, who distinguished himself at the Battle of Antietam. The statue was dedicated at the intersection of Connecticut and Florida Avenues on May 2, 1907.

CONNECTICUT AVENUE { PRESENT }

Today, Connecticut Avenue is lined with grand apartment buildings and ornate hotels, many built in 1920s and 1930s. Of special interest are the Kennedy-Warren Apartments, built in 1931 in Aztec Art Deco architectural style. The Wardman Tower—built in 1928 and now on the National Register of Historic Places—is still the city's largest hotel and was the home to three U.S. Presidents: Herbert Hoover, Dwight D. Eisenhower, and Lyndon B. Johnson. There is a great deal of diversity along the avenue with a variety of architectural styles, theaters, shops, parks, and many restaurants.

DUPONT CIRCLE { PAST }

Originally called Pacific Circle, Dupont Circle was renamed in 1884 to honor Admiral Samuel F. du Pont, who provided the Union with its first naval victory in the Civil War—an 1861 attack on the Confederate fortifications at Port Royal Harbor in South Carolina. In 1921, the du Pont family replaced the admiral's bronze statue with the marble fountain designed by Daniel Chester French. The three allegorical figure carvings represent the sea, wind, and stars. By the early 20th century, Dupont Circle was the desired address of Washington's captains of industry and moneyed elite.

The Patterson House (on the far right)—designed by noted architect Stanford White and built for *Chicago Tribune* publisher Robert Patterson—is the only remaining original mansion on the circle. The 1960s saw Dupont become a hangout for hippies and political activists, and the area fell on harder economic times until a restoration movement began in the 1980s. As during the beginning of the 20th century, Dupont Circle is now home to fine residences, galleries, restaurants, and the city's most frequented neighborhood park.

CAIRO APARTMENT BUILDING { PAST }

At 165 feet tall, the thirteen-story Cairo Apartment Building created an uproar when it opened in 1894, prompting Congress to pass an 1899 law limiting the height of buildings in the District of Columbia. Groundbreaking for its time, the Cairo was billed as the biggest, most luxurious building of its type in the city. It boasted a rooftop garden complete with fountains, a bakery, and all the late 19th century's most modern conveniences.

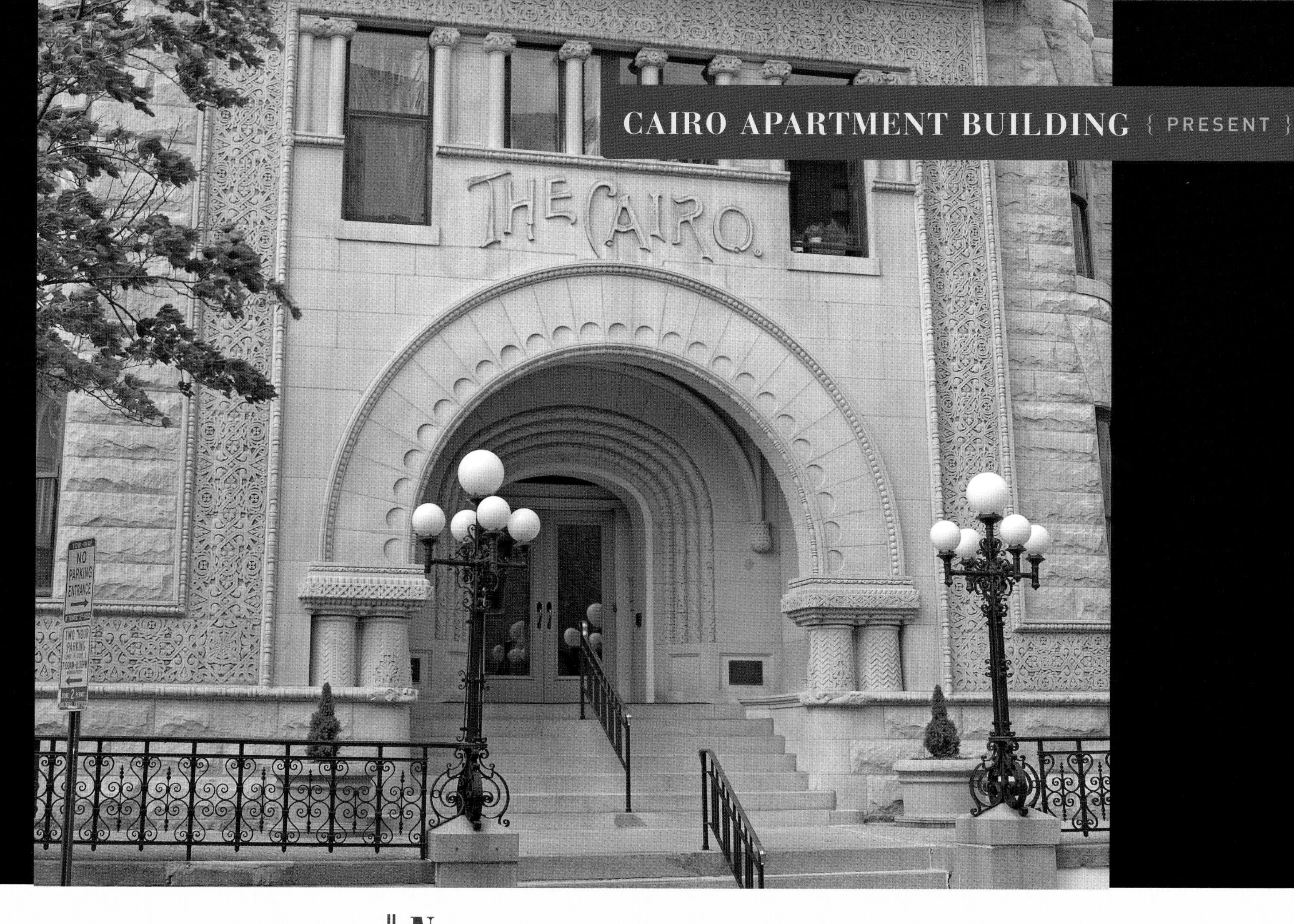

CAIRO APARTMENT BUILDING { PRESENT }

No longer an apartment building, today the Cairo features condominiums in the fashionable Dupont Circle neighborhood. Although there have been quite a few changes and additions to the building over the past century—including a complete interior renovation in 1976—the exterior of the Cairo remains substantially as Thomas Franklin Schneider originally designed it. In particular, the main entrance, with its exotic Moorish design, remains one of the Cairo's most eye-catching features.

TAFT BRIDGE { PAST }

Begun in 1897 and completed ten years later, the Connecticut Avenue Bridge was renamed the Taft Bridge, in honor of U.S. Supreme Court Chief Justice and President William Howard Taft, in 1931. At more than 900 feet long, this arch bridge, which carries Connecticut Avenue across the Rock Creek Valley and the Rock Creek and Potomac Parkways, is one of the world's largest non-reinforced concrete structures. Designed by George S. Morrison, the bridge was nicknamed "The Million Dollar Bridge," due to the enormous expense involved in its construction.

Each end of the Taft Bridge is anchored by a pair of massive concrete lions sculpted by Roland Hinton Perry. Unfortunately, concrete did not prove to be a durable material for this type of sculpture, so the lions have required careful maintenance and repairs over the decades. The bridge is also decorated with ten-foot-tall lampposts that line each side of the span. These cast-iron fixtures are topped with decorative eagles and were designed by sculptor Ernest C. Bairstow.

A City With a Plan

In 1777, 22-year-old, Parisian-born Pierre Charles L'Enfant arrived in the United States with Major General Lafayette to serve in the Continental Army, eventually becoming a Captain of Engineers on General George Washington's staff.

In the days and months that followed the war, there was much debate and political wrangling over where the new nation should install its federal government. In 1789, before Congress finalized any decisions, L'Enfant expressed his interest in plotting out the new capital to President Washington. L'Enfant had studied at the Royal Academy in the Louvre. After the war, he was professionally occupied in design and architecture, and his endeavors had provided him a fine reputation with a modicum of fame and fortune.

Washington ultimately selected a relatively uninhabited location along the Potomac River that straddled Virginia and Maryland and that was less than twenty miles north of his 8,000-acre Mount Vernon estate. Impressed with L'Enfant's ideas and hampered by the fact that there were very few city planners in the United States at that time, Washington appointed L'Enfant in 1791, giving him a clean slate with no permanent buildings, no established roadways, and no boundaries with which to contend for more than one hundred square miles.

L'Enfant had a wonderful vision of a beautiful city on a grand scale. He laid out a city for a population of 800,000 citizens. By comparison, Philadelphia was the young country's largest city in 1790 with a population of a little more than 28,500 residents. Growing up in Paris gave L'Enfant some practical konwledge of size and scale from which to project his plan. After his plans with its radiating avenues were released to the public, the *Maryland Journal* newspaper praised them as an "inconceivable improvement over all the cities of the world" (September 30, 1791).

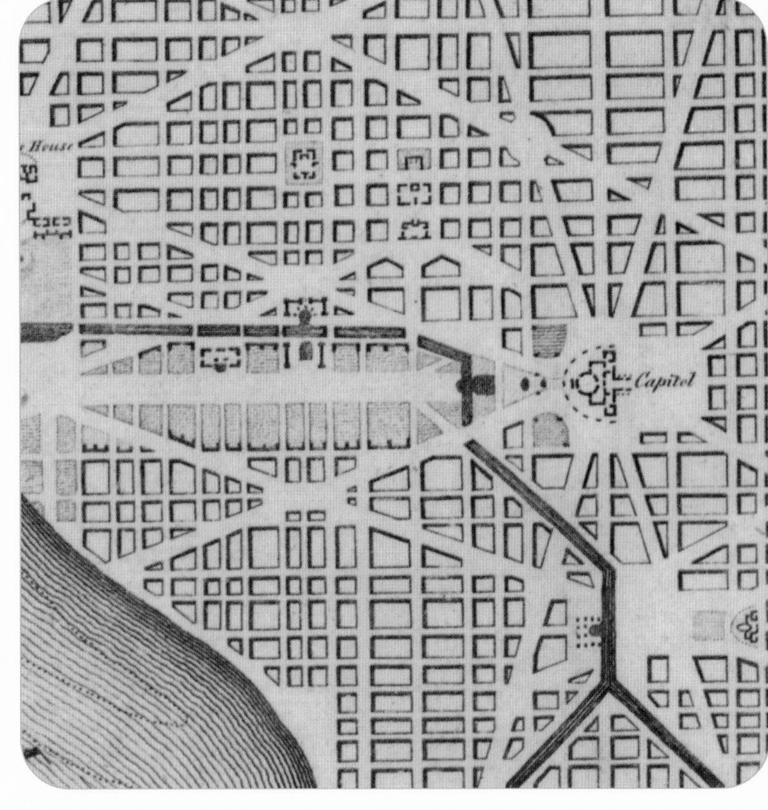

A CLOSE-UP OF L'ENFANT'S PLAN

The plans captured the spirit of democracy by positioning the seat of government at the center of it all. Every street directional (NW, SW, NE, SE) refers to its orientation with regards to the U.S. Capitol Building. (Had the new government been a monarchy, then the president's house would have been central.) L'Enfant's grid of long main thoroughfares, open spaces, the idea of a National Mall and the use of circles to set off communities within the city is still revered today.

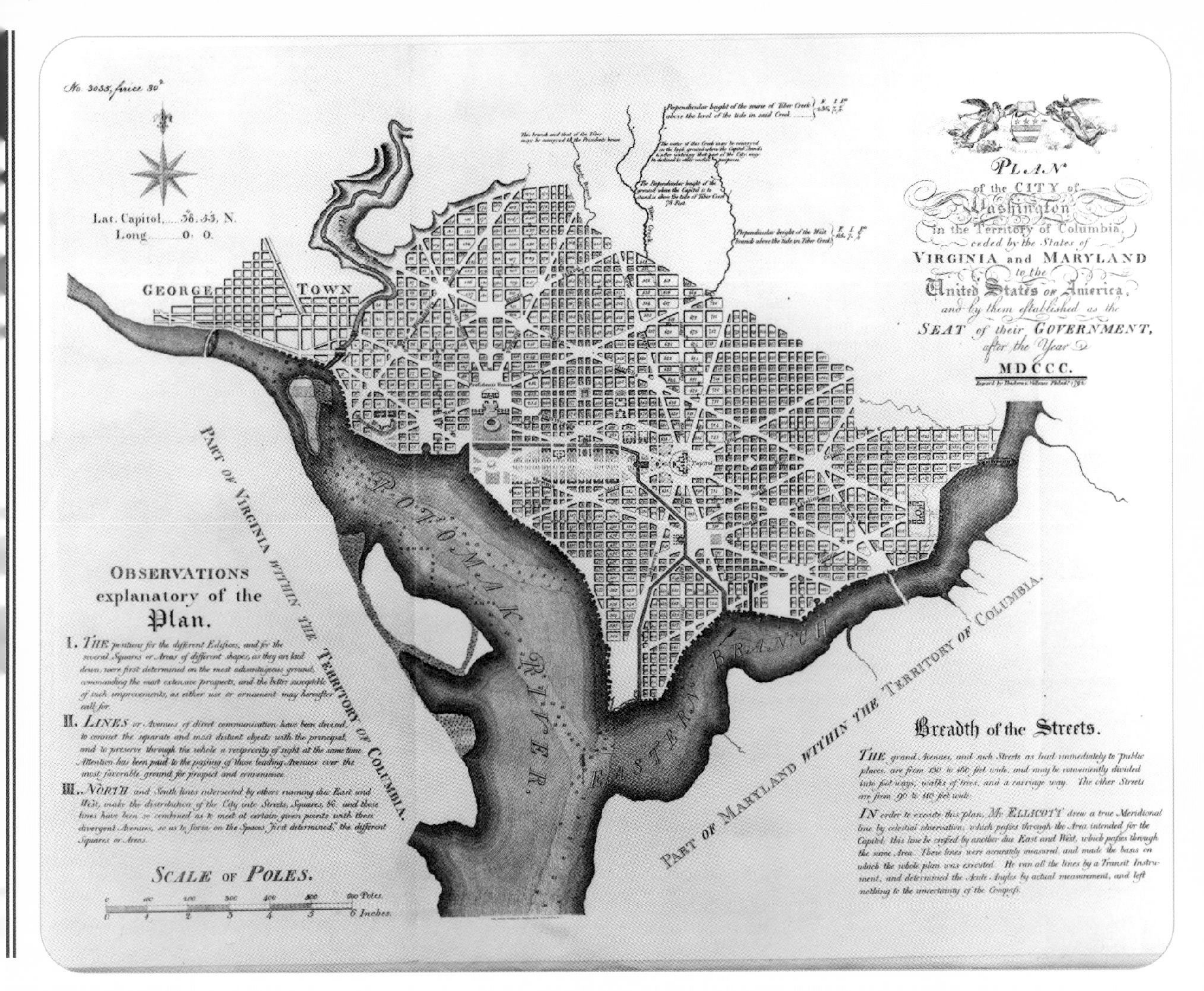

ELICOTT'S PLAN

Unfortunately, L'Enfant was unable to see his masterpiece through to completion. Perhaps the slow pace of the construction frustrated him, or perhaps he felt that no one else could see his city of tomorrow, or perhaps he let his importance go to his head, or perhaps his noted inability to compromise was to blame. Whatever the reason, his anger proved to be his downfall. After repeated attempts to resolve the issues L'Enfant had with the city's commissioners, President Washington was forced to dismiss the visionary in March 1792. The city planning was taken over by Andrew Ellicott, a land surveyor already working on the project.

L'Enfant was not paid for his work and felt disgraced. To gain back his honor, he spent much of the rest of his life trying to persuade Congress to pay him what he felt he was owed.

Sadly, Pierre Charles L'Enfant died in poverty in 1825 and was buried at the farm of a friend in Prince George's County, Maryland. In 1909, L'Enfant's remains were moved and fittingly buried in Arlington National Cemetery. The location of his grave is on a high spot in front of Robert E. Lee's Arlington House, which provides the best view of Washington from across the river.

PIERRE L'ENFANT'S TOMB

NATIONAL ZOO { PAST }

The Department of Living Animals, the precursor to the National Zoo, was created in 1887 and displayed various North American mammals in the area between the Capitol and the Lincoln Memorial (now known as the National Mall). In 1889, Congress set aside land along Rock Creek to create a national zoo. The project came under the management of the Smithsonian a year later, and the National Zoo officially opened in 1891. The 163-acre zoo was designed by renowned landscape architect Frederick Law Olmstead, the planner of Central Park in New York City.

NATIONAL ZOO { PRESENT }

The National Zoo is home to approximately 2,700 animals representing 435 different species—nearly one-third are on the world's endangered species list. Endangered animals on exhibit include Asian elephants, golden lion tamarins, Sumatran tigers, and Komodo dragons. Since 1971, the National Zoo has been home to giant pandas on loan from China. The zoo celebrated the birth of a male panda named Tai Shan (Peaceful Mountain) on July 9, 2005.

WASHINGTON NATIONAL CATHEDRAL { PAST }

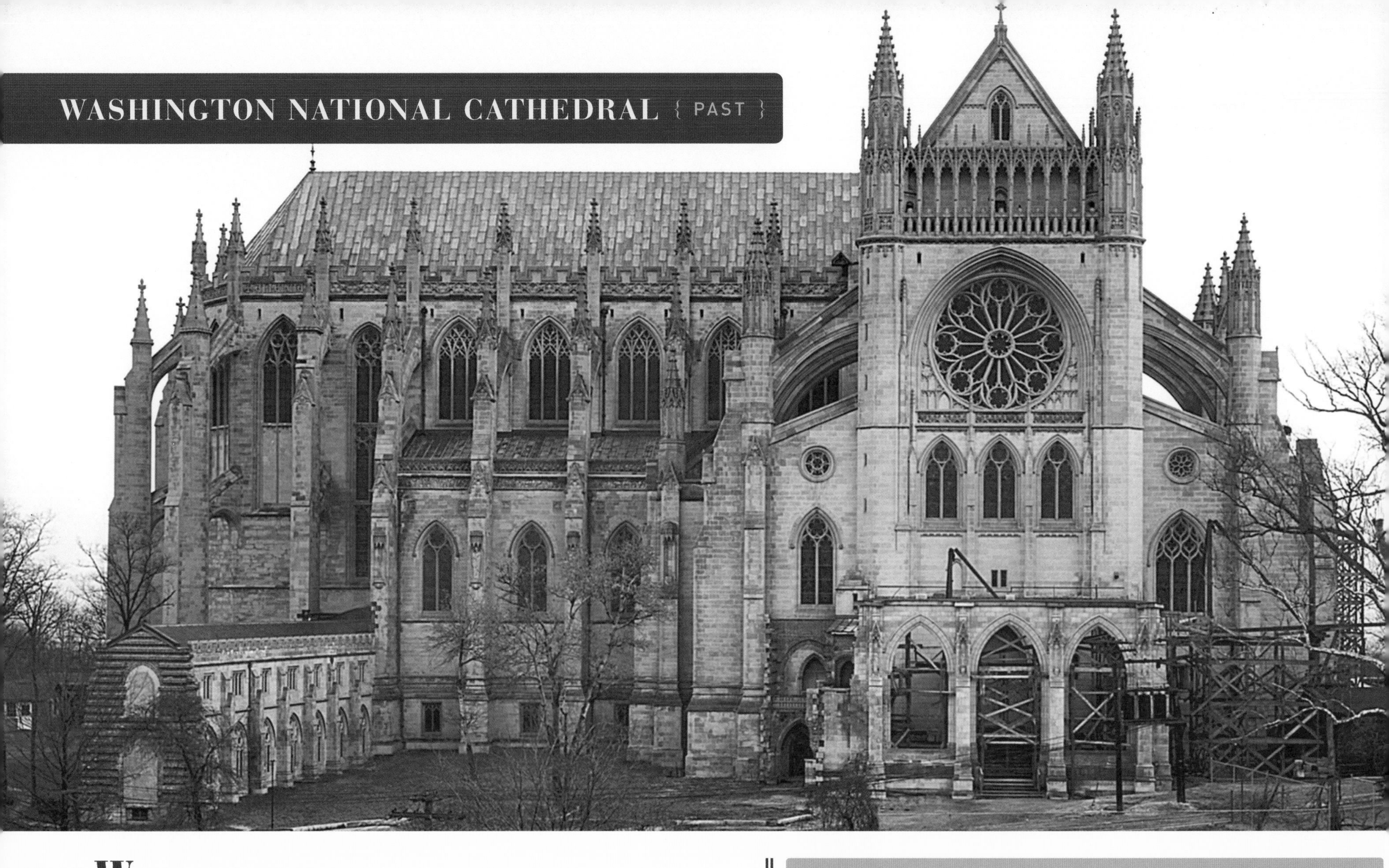

With the official name of The Cathedral Church of Saint Peter and Saint Paul in the City and Diocese of Washington, the National Cathedral is the sixth-largest cathedral in the world. The first services began in 1912 and have continued daily since, interrupted only by war or financial difficulties. Chief architect Phillip T. Frohman dedicated more than fifty years of his life to the project, from 1921 to 1972. No public funds were used to pay for the building as $65 million in private donations were raised for its construction.

LORE & LEGEND

According to the Bureau of Standards, the 150,000 tons of Indiana limestone used in the construction of the National Cathedral should last 2,000 years.

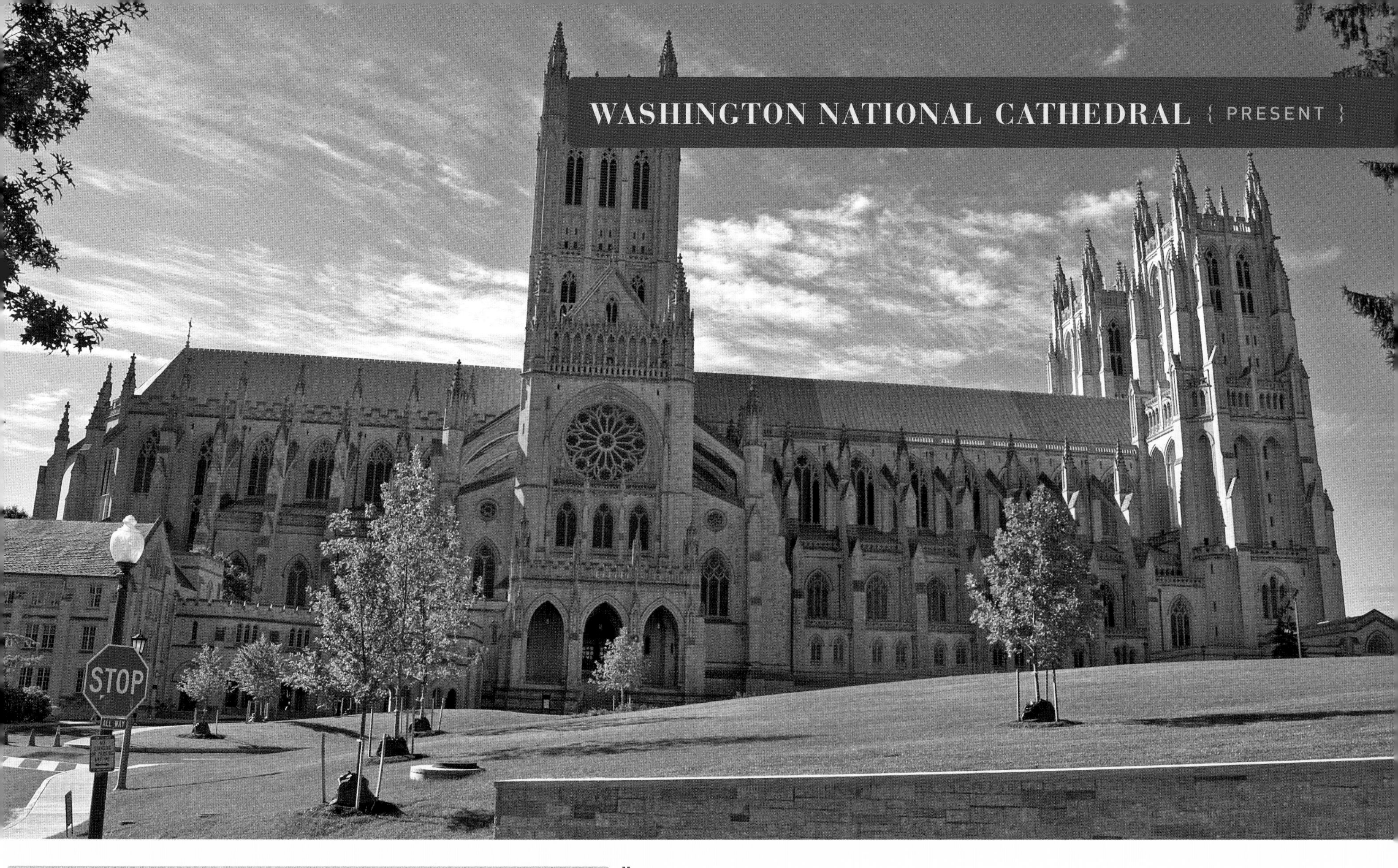

WASHINGTON NATIONAL CATHEDRAL { PRESENT }

LORE & LEGEND

A window on the south aisle of the Cathedral contains a piece of lunar rock that was donated by astronauts Neil Armstrong, Edwin "Buzz" Aldrin, and Michael Collins, the crew of *Apollo XI*. The Space Window was dedicated on April 21, 1974, the fifth anniversary of their lunar landing,

Although the church is the seat of the Washington Episcopal Diocese, it has no standing congregation and gladly accepts all denominations. On March 31, 1968, Dr. Martin Luther King Jr. preached his last Sunday sermon here. Sadly, just five days later, a memorial service for the slain Civil Rights leader was held in the cathedral. More than 150 people are interred here, including President Woodrow Wilson and Helen Keller. The cathedral was finally completed in 1990 with President George H.W. Bush presiding over the ceremony.

bassy Row refers to a stretch of Massachusetts Avenue—extending from Dupont Circle ward the National Cathedral—along which many of the city's foreign embassies are located. icture, taken around 1907, is of the Christian Hauge House, designed by the Parisian-trained ican architect George Oakley Totten Jr. Christian Hauge was Norway's first minister to the d States, and he used the building as both his residence and his native country's American Hauge died accidentally in 1908, but his American wife maintained the residence for er nineteen years. The building later became the embassy of Czechoslovakia.

Totten ultimately designed four buildings along Massachusetts Avenue, including the cu Turkish and Pakistani embassies. The Hauge mansion is now the Embassy of the Repub Cameroon, which purchased the building in 1972. It is architecturally significant as it is the finest example of Chateauesque style. With the separation of the former Soviet Union Yugoslavia into smaller, self-governed states, embassies for Croatia, Armenia, Kazakhstan others have been established in the capital. There are currently more than 170 foreign emba in Washington, D.C., but none representing Iran, Iraq, or Cuba.

LOGAN CIRCLE { PAST }

Until the Civil War, the area that was originally called Iowa Circle was still mostly farmland and open fields. During the Civil War, freedmen and vagrants built shanties in the open space, which also became a spot where military deserters and spies were executed. After the war, however, the circle was developed into a desirable residential location, eventually becoming a neighborhood where African-American culture thrived. In 1930, Congress passed legislation that renamed the circle after John A. Logan, a Civil War general and senator from Illinois.

LORE & LEGEND

In the 1910s, many of the circle's homes we
and replaced by car dealerships, turning 14
what was called "Automobile Row."

LOGAN CIRCLE { PRESENT }

In the 1950s, Logan Circle fell into disrepair after years of neglect. During the 1970s, however, the area experienced a revitalization, with many of the stately mansions undergoing extensive renovations—some rehabilitated to their original splendor. In 1972, Logan Circle was added to the National Register of Historic Places. Today, the area continues to thrive, with the National Park Service planning a significant renovation of Logan Circle Park.

GEORGETOWN UNIVERSITY { PAST }

In 1789, Georgetown College became the country's first Catholic institution of higher learning. The son of an Irish immigrant and a former slave, Father Patrick Healy became the first African-American to earn a PhD and the first to head what is today a major American research university. He expanded the curriculum, improved studies in science, and constructed a new building—later known as Healy Hall, above—with laboratories, library, classrooms, dormitory rooms, and a meeting space for alumni.

LORE & LEGEND

Of the 1,141 Georgetown alumni and students who fought in the Civil War, 925 joined the Confederate ranks. After the war, the school adopted blue and gray as its official colors to symbolize the reunification of the North and the South.

During the late 1960s, the school began admitting women to its College of Arts and Sciences. Over the years, Georgetown University has grown from a small academy to a highly regarded university with a student body of around 12,000 coming from all fifty states and more than one hundred countries. A notable sampling of Georgetown University alumni includes: President William J. Clinton; U.S. Supreme Court Justice Antonin Scalia; broadcast journalist Maria Shriver; Project Hope founder William Walsh; author William Peter Blatty; and basketball star Patrick Ewing.

CHESAPEAKE AND OHIO (C&O) CANAL { PAST }

Until the advent of the railroad, water travel was far superior to land travel—in fact, the practice of transporting goods by man-made waterways dates back to ancient times. The Chesapeake and Ohio (C&O) Canal was originally planned to stretch more than 450 miles northwest to Pittsburgh, where it was to join the Ohio River. Construction began in 1828 and halted for good in 1850, though the canal was less than half completed. The seventy-five lift locks used in the C&O Canal's construction were an adaptation of a Leonardo da Vinci design from the late 15th century.

CHESAPEAKE AND OHIO (C&O) CANAL { PRESENT }

U.S. Supreme Court Justice William O. Douglas, a key supporter of the fledgling environmental movement, saved the canal's towpath from being paved and made into a road. And the entire 184.5-mile canal—which stretches from Georgetown to Cumberland, Maryland—was designated a National Historic Park in 1971. Today, millions of visitors hike, bike, or camp along the C&O Canal each year. Starting each April through early fall, locals and tourists can take a leisurely "cruise" on the *Georgetown*, a replica 19th-century canal boat powered by a mule that travels at a top speed of four miles per hour.

FRANCIS SCOTT KEY MANSION { PAST }

The Key Mansion was the home and office of Francis Scott Key, who lived there from 1803 to around 1833. Key, a well-respected lawyer in Georgetown, is most famous for penning "The Star-Spangled Banner" (originally called "The Defence of Fort McHenry"). After witnessing the British Navy bombarding Fort McHenry, Key was so moved upon seeing the American flag on the morning of September 14, 1814, that he began to write what would eventually become the national anthem. This photograph was taken in 1908.

Key's poem was soon after set to a popular tune and came to represent the country's indomitable spirit. In 1916, President Woodrow Wilson declared it the Armed Forces' official anthem. On March 3, 1931, President Herbert Hoover signed the law making "The Star-Spangled Banner" the official national anthem. Sadly, Key's house was demolished in 1947 after years of neglect by various private owners. The Francis Scott Key Park now honors the patriot poet and is near the site of the former mansion.

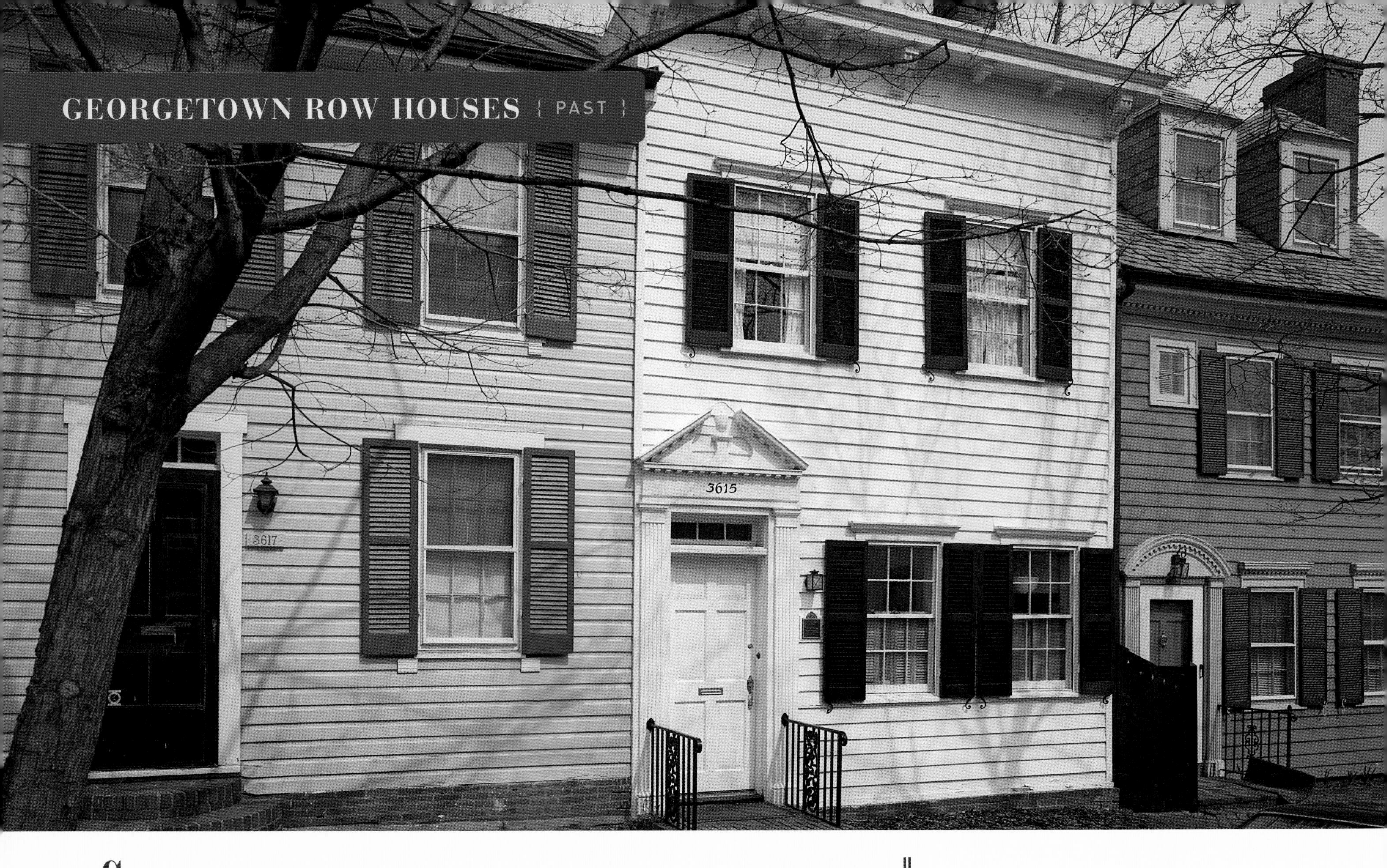

Georgetown—a port location along the Potomac River—was founded about forty years before the capital city. The Chesapeake and Ohio Canal was to have cemented Georgetown's importance as a place of commerce, but the canal was never completed due to emergence of an extensive railway system. Thereafter, Georgetown became a poor neighbor of Washington and was eventually annexed by the capital in 1871. With lessened importance came less expensive real estate. The 1850s row houses pictured here along O Street were sold quite cheaply.

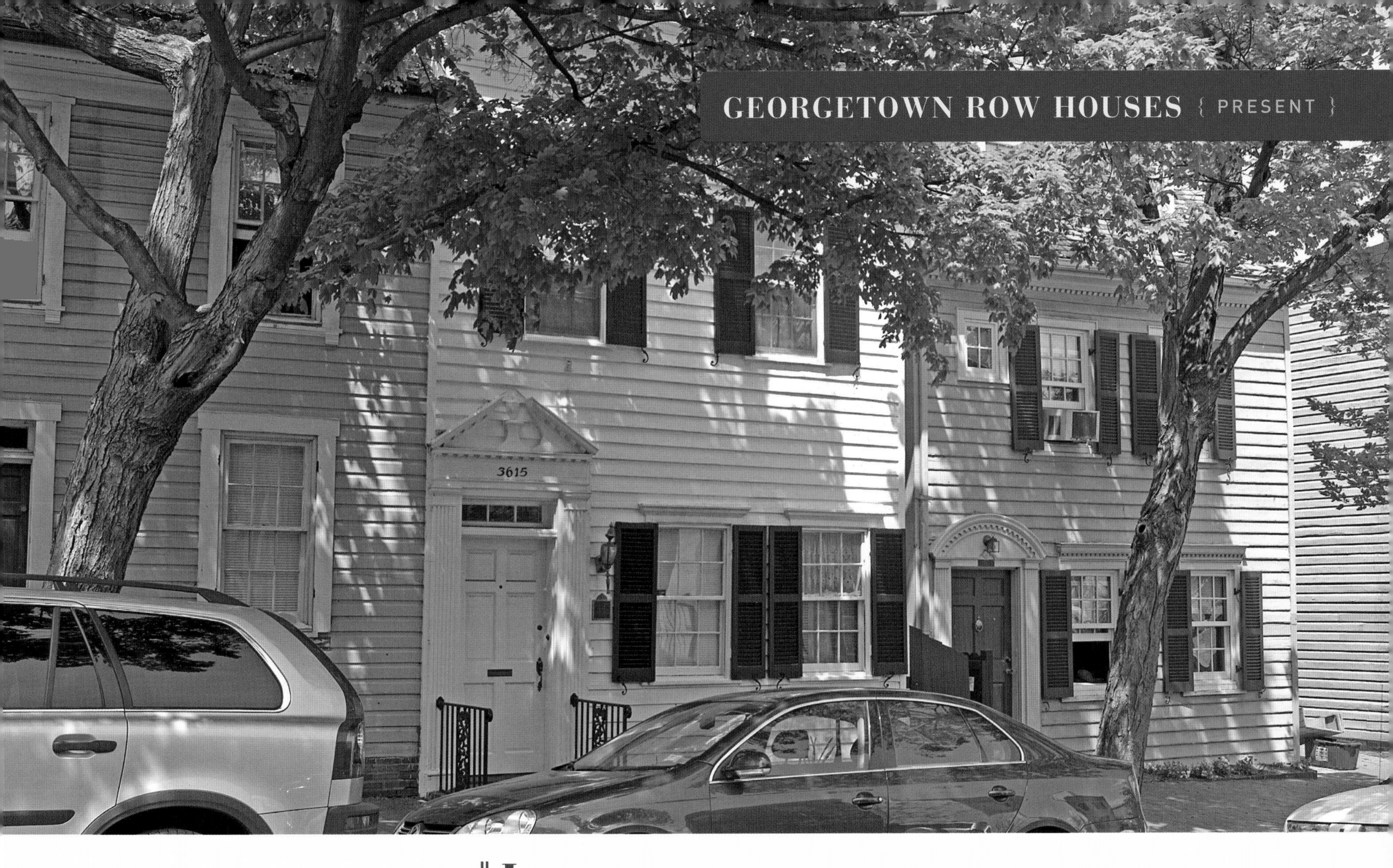

In the 1950s, Georgetown underwent a transformation and was added to the National Register of Historic Places. What was once small and inexpensive housing was soon described as quaint and charming—and in demand. Prices of modest 19th-century residences soared into the six-figure range and even higher. Many of the houses have become chic shops, while others have the distinction of being the homes of past and present history makers.

OLD STONE HOUSE { PAST }

Generations of Washingtonians have grown up hearing the legend of George Washington and Pierre Charles L'Enfant meeting at the Old Stone House to lay out the design for the District of Columbia. Although the story is now believed to be untrue, the Old Stone House is nonetheless a historically significant building. Built in 1765 by cabinetmaker Christopher Layman, the charming little house is the oldest surviving building in the District. When the National Park Service purchased the building in the 1950s, it was serving as the office for a used car lot.

OLD STONE HOUSE { PRESENT }

Since then, the Old Stone House has been carefully restored to its original condition. The portions of the building that are open to the public are filled with 18th-century artifacts and reproductions of common household and work objects. These displays give visitors a view of everyday life in the second half of the 18th century. Although renovated, the house still features the floors, paneling, and stone walls that are original to the house.

FRANCIS SCOTT KEY BRIDGE { PAST }

In a city filled with buildings that hearken back to ancient Rome and Greece, it is only natural that one of the main bridges into Washington would echo the design and look of a Roman viaduct. The five curving arches of the 1,650-foot-long Francis Scott Key Bridge were designed by architect Nathan C. Wyeth and built by the U.S. Army Corps of Engineers. Opened to traffic in 1923, the bridge was named after Francis Scott Key, author of the "The Star Spangled Banner," whose home was located near the Georgetown side of the span.

FRANCIS SCOTT KEY BRIDGE { PRESENT }

The Key Bridge remains one of the most important arteries linking Washington and Northern Virginia. Offering an exceptionally scenic view of the Potomac River for the thousands of vehicles and pedestrians that cross it each day, the Key Bridge is a popular choice for visitors seeking a quick route into Georgetown, an upscale District neighborhood that features some of the city's best restaurants and shopping. Commuters traveling out of the District find that the bridge provides them with fast access to the office buildings of Rosslyn, one of Northern Virginia's most active business districts.

ARLINGTON NATIONAL CEMETERY { PAST }

Shortly after Robert E. Lee left his home to lead Virginia's volunteers and serve in the Confederate Army, the federal government confiscated his 1,100-acre estate that overlooked the Potomac River from its western bank, turning part of the plantation into a cemetery. Private William Christman of Pennsylvania was the first soldier interred there on May 13, 1864, and by the end of the Civil War, nearly 16,000 Union soldiers had been laid to rest in Arlington. The graveyard, however, did not become the country's national cemetery until 1883. Pictured here is the 1920 burial service of Miss Jane Delano, a famed Army and Red Cross nurse.

ARLINGTON NATIONAL CEMETERY { PRESENT }

LORE & LEGEND

Among those interred at Arlington National Cemetery are astronaut Virgil "Gus" Grissom; heavyweight champion Joe Louis; author Dashiell Hammett; explorers Matthew Henson and Robert Peary; U.S. Supreme Court Justice Thurgood Marshall; and Brigadier General Abner Doubleday, the inventor of baseball.

Veterans from every armed conflict since the Revolutionary War have been laid to rest at Arlington National Cemetery. Pre–Civil War soldiers were re-interred here in the 20th century. Among the 300,000 people buried here are nearly 5,000 unknowns and sixty-three foreign nationals who fought and died for American causes. The memorial park receives four million visitors each year, and a daily procession of between twenty-five and thirty funerals takes place each weekday. Current projections show that the 612-acre burial grounds will be filled to capacity by the year 2025.

KENNEDY GRAVESITE { PAST }

President John F. Kennedy made his first formal visit to Arlington National Cemetery on Armistice Day in November 1961. Three days after his assassination on November 22, 1963, Kennedy was interred at Arlington. In this photograph, John F. Kennedy Jr. places a "PT-109" tie clasp on his father's grave as mother, Jacqueline, and sister, Caroline, watch with a host of other mourners. During the following year, more than 3,000 people visited the site each hour.

KENNEDY GRAVESITE { PRESENT }

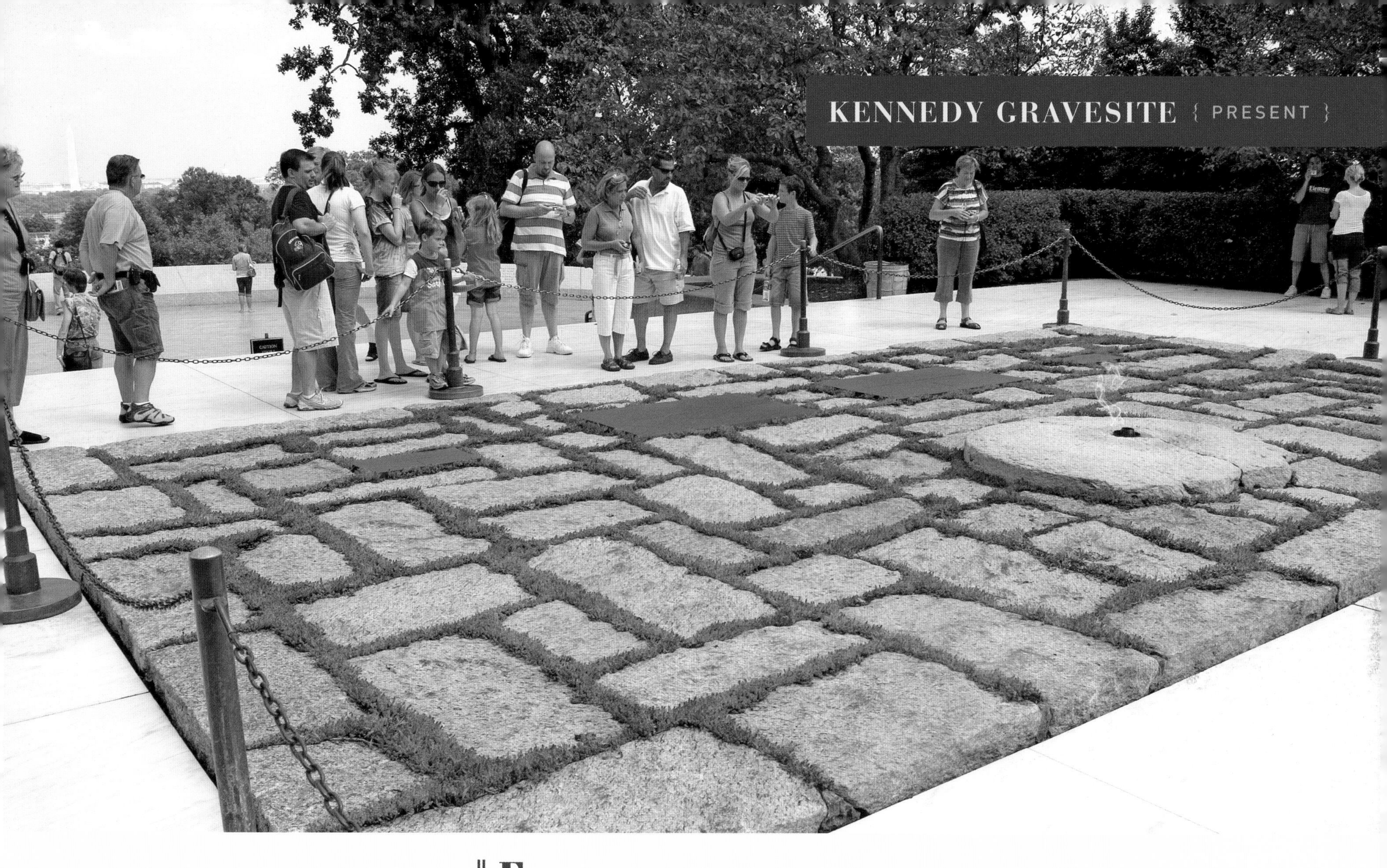

Eventually, irregular stones of Cape Cod granite were set, clover and sedum were planted, and the picket fence was removed from around the grave. The eternal flame, lit by Jacqueline Kennedy on the day of her husband's funeral, still burns brightly today. Nearby, a white wooden cross marks the grave of the late president's younger brother, Robert F. Kennedy, who was assassinated on June 5, 1968. On May 23, 1994, Jacqueline Bouvier Kennedy Onassis was laid to rest next to her first husband.

A City of Speeches

When a president speaks on war or peace, human rights or human misgivings, the topic and the politics of the day are spoken of in grand and eloquent words. The city of Washington has long remembered the whens and wheres of these and many other speeches.

"Seventy-five dollars per head! Fifteen thousand three hundred and seventy-five dollars for two hundred and five men and women! What a revolution in the relative value of slaves and of freemen, since the age of Homer! In the estimate of that Prince of Grecian Poets: 'Jove fix't it certain that whatever day Makes man a slave, takes half his worth away.'"

John Quincy Adams addressed the Supreme Court in the Amistad case on March 1, 1841, as a lawyer for the defense. Adams had already served as president and was a congressman from Massachusetts at the time of the case. The court ruled in his favor.

"I have no purpose, directly or indirectly, to interfere with the institution of slavery in the States where it exists. I believe I have no lawful right to do so, and I have no inclination to do so."

President Abraham Lincoln said these words during his first Inaugural Address, March 4, 1861, from the Capitol. Lincoln would sign the Emancipation Proclamation less than two years later.

"This great Nation will endure as it has endured, will revive and will prosper. So, first of all, let me assert my firm belief that the only thing we have to fear is fear itself—nameless, unreasoning, unjustified terror which paralyzes needed efforts to convert retreat into advance."

JOHN QUINCY ADAMS

HARRY S. TRUMAN

LINCOLN'S INAUGURATION

President Franklin D. Roosevelt from the East Portico of the Capitol in his first Inaugural Address, March 4, 1933. Under FDR's leadership, the country endured the hardships of the Great Depression and World War II, after which it began to revive and prosper again.

FRANKLIN D. ROOSEVELT

RONALD REAGAN

JIMMY CARTER

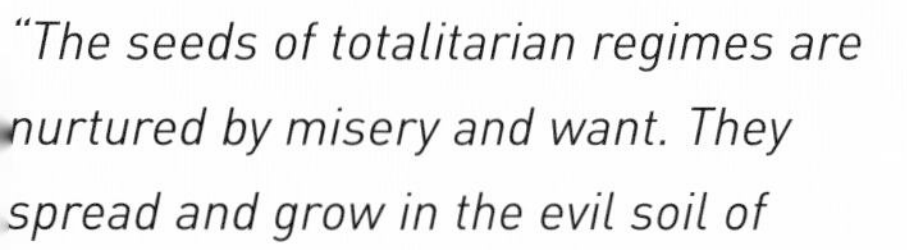

"The seeds of totalitarian regimes are nurtured by misery and want. They spread and grow in the evil soil of poverty and strife. They reach their full growth when the hope of a people for a better life has died."

President Harry S. Truman spoke his doctrine before Congress on March 12, 1947, requesting aid for weakened Greece and Turkey to stop the global spread of Communism.

"It is the effort of American Negroes to secure for themselves the full blessings of American life. Their cause must be our cause too. Because it is not just Negroes, but really it is all of us, who must overcome the crippling legacy of bigotry and injustice. And we shall overcome."

President Lyndon Johnson before Congress on March 15, 1965. Johnson signed the Voting Rights Act that year and the Civil Rights Act in 1968.

"In an all-out nuclear war, more destructive power than in all of World War II would be unleashed every second for the long afternoon it would take for all the missiles and bombs to fall. A World War II every second—more people killed in the first few hours than all the wars of history put together. The survivors, if any, would live in despair amid poisoned ruins of a civilization that had committed suicide."

President Jimmy Carter, in his Farewell Address, January 14, 1981. Carter received the Nobel Peace Prize in 2002.

"The defense policy of the United States is based on a simple premise: the United States does not start fights. We will never be an aggressor. We maintain our strength in order to deter and defend against aggression—to preserve freedom and peace."

President Ronald Reagan on March 23, 1983, announcing the Strategic Defense Initiative, which marked the last phase of the Cold War.

TOMB OF THE UNKNOWNS { PAST }

"Here Rests in Honored Glory An American Soldier Known but to God." On November 11, 1921, the remains of an unknown American soldier from World War I were interred at Arlington National Cemetery during a ceremony attended by President Warren G. Harding, General John J. Pershing, Chief Plenty Coup, and a host of other dignitaries and notables. In succeeding years, the remains of other Unknowns from World War II, the Korean War, and the Vietnam War were also interred at the site, which has become one of the most sacred shrines to American military service.

TOMB OF THE UNKNOWNS { PRESENT }

A perpetual honor guard was established for the tomb in 1937, and eleven years later, the soldiers of the 3rd United States Infantry, known as "The Old Guard," were permanently assigned the honor of guarding the Tomb of the Unknowns. In 1998, the remains of the Vietnam War Unknown were identified as those of Captain Michael Blassie and removed for private burial. The Vietnam crypt has since remained empty. Advances in DNA testing and identification make it highly unlikely that any more Unknowns will be interred at Arlington in the future.

ARLINGTON HOUSE / THE ROBERT E. LEE MEMORIAL { PAST }

George Washington Parke Custis built Arlington House in the Greek Revival style to be both his home and a memorial to President George Washington, his step-grandfather, who had raised him after his own father died. Built of cement-covered brick by slaves between 1802 and 1818, the house later became the home of Robert E. Lee when he married G.W.P. Custis' only surviving child, Mary Anna, in 1831. Lee and his family lived here for thirty years until the Civil War began and they left for Richmond, Virginia. Records show that General Lee never returned to Arlington after the war.

ARLINGTON HOUSE / THE ROBERT E. LEE MEMORIAL { PRESENT }

The will of G.W.P. Custis passed the land from his daughter to her first-born son, George Washington Custis Lee, who fought and won a legal battle to reclaim his family's estate after his mother's death in 1873. G.W.C. Lee won the court battle and the title to the property. He eventually sold it back to the U.S. government for $150,000. The Custis-Lee mansion is now preserved as a memorial to General Lee, who had gained the admiration of Americans from both sides of the battlefield.

ARLINGTON MEMORIAL BRIDGE { PAST }

Built between 1926 and 1932, Arlington Memorial Bridge crosses the Potomac River, linking the North and the South. On the north side of the bridge is the Lincoln Memorial, and the Robert E. Lee Memorial (Arlington House) is on the south side. This alignment was done with thoughtful intent to symbolically represent the country's reunification. Designed by the esteemed architectural firm McKim, Mead and White, the low, neoclassical bridge is 2,163 feet long.

ARLINGTON MEMORIAL BRIDGE { PRESENT }

Regarded as Washington's most beautiful span, the Arlington Memorial Bridge is one of the city's major traffic routes. At the east end of the bridge and the parkway are two pairs of equestrian sculpture on identical pedestals: *The Arts of War* by Leo Friedlander and *The Arts of Peace* by James Earle Fraser. Erected in 1951 and restored in 1971, the bronze statues were cast and gilded by Italy as a gift to the United States. The drawbridge mechanism, with its center span opening to allow large vessels upriver to Georgetown, is no longer used.

The design of the Pentagon was conceived out of practicality, as it conformed to the five-sided lot that was originally designated as the planned building site. President Franklin D. Roosevelt liked its look but not the proposed site, and selected a different location farther south of Arlington National Cemetery. With a workforce of round-the-clock shifts, the mammoth building took only sixteen months to complete. The War Department then combined the military and civilian personnel from seventeen offices scattered around Washington into this facility.

LORE & LEGEND

Under direct orders from the War Department, Architect George E. Bergstrom and army engineers successfully conceived of and produced the basic plans and perspectives for the Pentagon in one weekend.

LORE & LEGEND

To feed the town-sized population of the Pentagon's daily work force—approximately 24,000 people—the Pentagon has a total of ten restaurants, dining rooms, cafeterias, and snack bars, and has a food service staff of 230 people.

One of the largest and most recognizable office buildings in the world, the Pentagon was designated a National Historic Landmark in 1992. It has six and a half million square feet of floor space—three times that of the Empire State Building. A hijacked airliner struck the Pentagon on September 11, 2001, exactly sixty years to the day of the building's official groundbreaking. A $1.1 billion renovation of all five "wedges" is scheduled to be completed by 2014, and a memorial for the 184 victims of the terrorist attack is in development.

NATIONAL AIRPORT { PAST }

Once the captains of industry mastered building the machines of flight, they needed a place to land them. The first half of the 20th century showed a capital city with inadequate airports. In 1938, after years of congressional squabbling, President Franklin D. Roosevelt selected the location for a national airport: a place called Gravelly Point about four miles south of the city. As most of that location was underwater, engineers spent two years filling in the site. National Airport opened in June 1941. Within six months, airport operations were dominated by military uses because of World War II.

RONALD REAGAN WASHINGTON NATIONAL AIRPORT { PRESENT }

National Airport became a great success. Over the decades, runways were lengthened, and hangars and a North Terminal were added. In 1986, President Ronald Reagan transferred the operation of National Airport to a new regional Airports Authority. In 1997, Cesar Pelli's design of a new terminal transformed the look and efficiency of the airport. The new terminal has a scenic view of Washington and contains works of art (glass, marble, mosaic, terrazzo, and murals) from thirty artists incorporated into the structure. In 1998, President Bill Clinton signed the law that renamed the airport the Ronald Reagan Washington National Airport.

RICE, BIRCH & CO. SLAVE DEALERS { PAST }

Although the slave trade ended in the District of Columbia in 1850, slavery itself continued to exist until April 16, 1862, when President Lincoln signed emancipation documents freeing the district's slaves. A vigorous slave trade continued to flourish in Virginia and Maryland. Just across the river from the capital, Alexandria was the home of many slave dealers, the most notorious of whom, James Birch of Price, Birch & Co. and Joseph Bruin of Bruin & Hill, operated slave pens on Duke Street.

FORMER OFFICE OF PRICE, BIRCH & CO. SLAVE DEALERS { PRESENT }

At the commencement of the Civil War, the Union Army captured Alexandria and put an end to the trade in human beings conducted by slave dealers. The slave pen at Price, Birch & Co., with its dark, primitive cells, was put to use as a jail for drunk and disorderly soldiers. It was also an object of curiosity for visiting soldiers, who came to see the conditions in which slaves had been held. The building was used as a courthouse until 1865, and today it is a privately owned office building.

Constructed between 1958 and 1961, the Woodrow Wilson Memorial Bridge is fittingly named after President Wilson, who signed the Road-Aid Act of 1916 that created the federal-aid highway program. The bridge is part of the Capital Beltway (a highway), which circles the entire city of Washington. The original plans for the lightweight drawbridge did not anticipate that the bridge would soon become a major route for both local resident commuters and travelers heading up and down the East Coast.

WOODROW WILSON MEMORIAL BRIDGE { PRESENT }

By the mid-1980s, the bridge was carrying more than twice its intended load, and the critical need for a more substantial crossing became apparent. Since 2000, two side-by-side drawbridges with a total of twelve lanes have been under construction. The new, taller bridge is formed by a series of V-shaped piers linked by beams that combine to form faux arches. The old Wilson Bridge was demolished in August 2006, and the entire project is scheduled to be completed by 2009.

MOUNT VERNON { PAST }

Located sixteen miles south of the nation's capital on the Virginia side of the Potomac River, Mount Vernon was the estate of George Washington's family. Lord Culpeper granted the property to Washington's great-grandfather, John, in 1674. Washington's elder half-brother, Lawrence, named the 2,500-acre estate in 1740. Over the years, George added land parcels, which grew his holdings to include 8,000 acres with five farms and 300 slaves. Though the country's first president loved being a farmer, the rigors of military duty and public service kept him from that occupation and his home for considerable portions of his adult life.

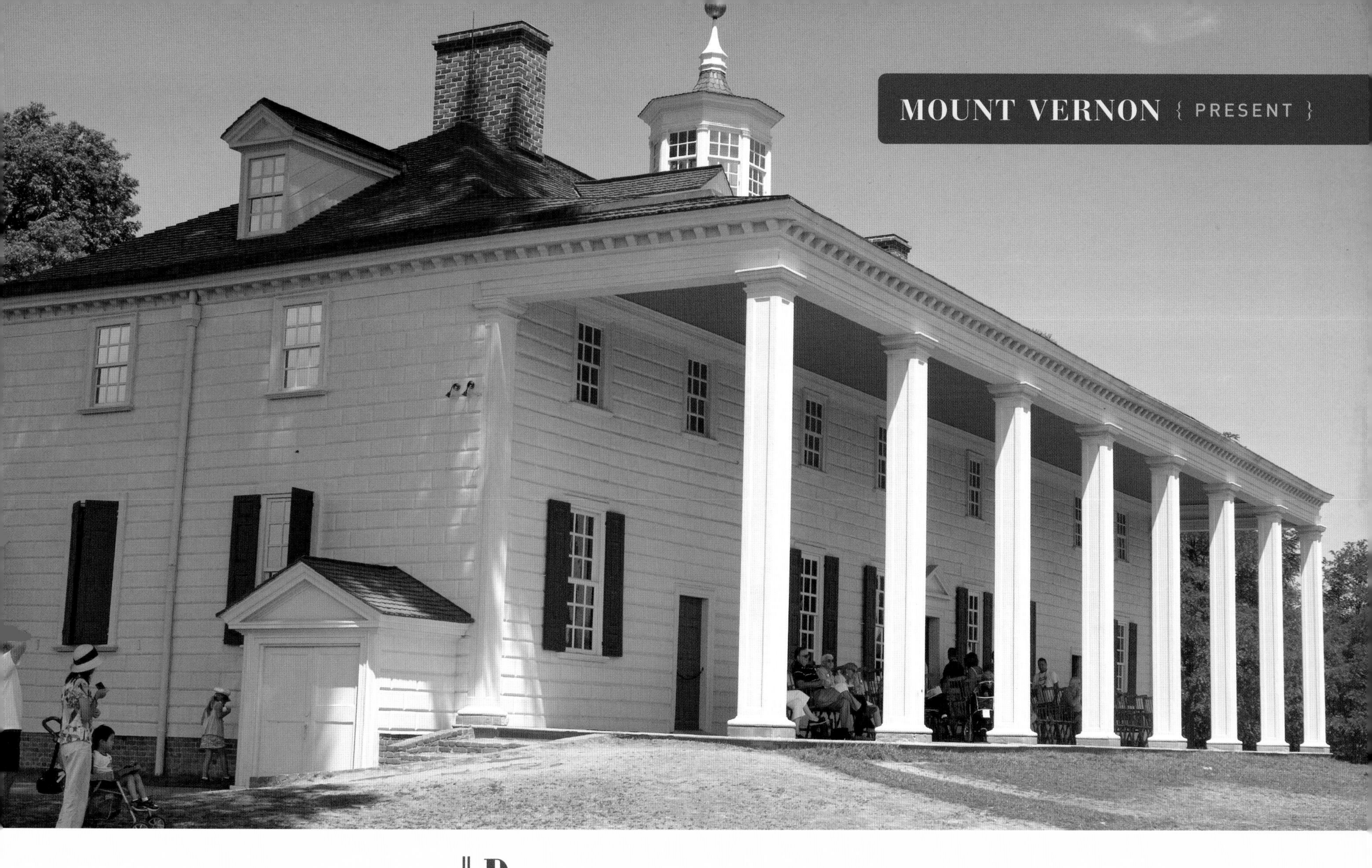

MOUNT VERNON { PRESENT }

Reduced in size to a well-tended 500 acres, Mount Vernon is now privately owned and administered and is the country's most visited historic estate. It's hard to believe that the grand Georgian-style mansion was once a modest farmhouse. Over time, the president raised the roof to two-and-a-half stories and added north and south wings and later the large dining room and the "piazza." The towering porch is on the back side of the house, which faces the river. The house is decorated in period furnishings, with original and period artifacts including the four-poster bed where Washington passed away. In addition to the main house, there are gardens, a nursery, museums, and a slave memorial on the grounds.

Resources for Further Exploration

Access Washington, D.C.
Richard Saul Wurman
9th edition updates by Beth Luberecki
HarperResource
New York 2005

Adams Morgan: Then & Now
Celestino Zapata and Josh Gibosn
Arcadia Publishing
Mount Pleasant, South Carolina 2006

America's First Families:
An Inside View of 200 Years of Private Life in the White House
Carl Sferrazza Anthony
Touchstone, a division of Simon & Schuster
New York 2000

Off the Beaten Path: Washington, D.C.
William Whitman, 3rd edition
Insider's Guide, an imprint of Globe Pequot
Guilford, Connecticut 2005

Real Life at the White House:
200 Years of Daily Life at America's Most Famous Residence
John Whitcomb and Claire Whitcomb
Routledge
New York 2000

Washington: The Nation's Capital
Thomas G. and Virginia L. Aylesworth
Gallery Books, a division of W.H. Smith Publishers
New York 1986

Washington: Pride and Glory of America
Isabella Brega
Smithmark Publishers
New York 1997

Washington, D.C.: A Pictorial Celebration
Jean Fogle
Sterling Publishing Co., Inc.
New York 2005

Washington, D.C.: A Smithsonian Book of the Nation's Capital
Smithsonian Books
Washington, D.C. 1992

www.loc.gov
The Library of Congress Web site gives you access to the world's largest library.

www.nps.org
The National Park Service Web site has information on the many monuments, memorials, museums, and parks within Washington, D.C., that are under its management. It is a good place to check for visiting hours or last-minute schedule changes if you plan to visit.

ndex

Index (continued)

Photo Credits

Gil King: pp. 11, 13, 15, 17, 23, 25, 27, 29, 31, 33, 35, 39, 41, 43, 45, 47, 49, 51, 53, 55, 57, 59, 63, 65, 67, 69, 71, 73, 75, 77, 79, 80 (bottom right), 81 (bottom right), 83, 85, **87**, 89, 91, 93, 95, 97, 99 (bottom right), 101, 103, 105, 109, 111, 113, 115, 117, 119, 121, 123, 127, 131, 133, 137, 139, 141

Courtesy of the Library of Congress: pp. 2, 6, 10, 12, 14, 16, 18, 21 (left & right), 24, 26, 30, 32, 34, 36 (left & right), 37 (left & top right), 40, 42, 44, 48, 56, 58, 60 (left), 61, 72, 74, 76, 78, 80 (top left & right, bottom left), 81 (top left, top & bottom center), 82, 84, 86, 90, 92, 94, 96, 98 (left & right), 99 (left), 100, 102, 104, 106, 108, 110, 112, 114, 116, 120, 124–125, 126, 130, 134, 136, 138, 140

© Robert H. Creigh/shutterstock.com: p. 5

© Condor 36/shutterstock.com: p. 8

© Yan Zverev/shutterstock.com: p. 19

© Charlie Hutton/shutterstock.com: p. 20

National Gallery of Art, Gallery Archives, detail of photograph: p. 22

Smithsonian Institution Archives, Record Unit 95, image # 72-5114, detail of photograph: p. 28

© Steve Maehl/shutterstock.com: p. 37 (bottom right)

Courtesy of George Eastman House collection, Rochester, NY, detail of photographs by Charles C. Zoller: pp. 38, 140

© Wally McNamee/CORBIS: p. 46

Courtesy of the Kennedy Center Archive: p. 50

AP Images/Bob Daugherty: p. 52

AP Images/William J. Smith: p. 54

© Richard F. Cox/shutterstock.com: p. 60 (right)

Abbie Rowe, National Park Service, courtesy Harry S. Truman Library: p. 62

Courtesy of George Eastman House collection, Rochester, NY, detail of photograph: p. 64

Smithsonian Institution Archives, Record Unit 95, image # MAH-9498, detail of photograph: p. 66

Smithsonian Institution Archives, Record Unit 95, image # 85-4824, detail of photograph: p. 68

Smithsonian Institution Archives, Record Unit 95, image # MAH-48214B, detail of photograph: p. 70

The Historical Society of Washington, D.C., Wymer Collection WY2210.36, detail of photograph: p. 88

© Kim Seidl/shutterstock.com: p. 107

The Historical Society of Washington, D.C., postcard collection, PC BR .KY1, detail of postcard: p. 118

© Bettmann/CORBIS: p. 122

Courtesy of Picture History: p. 128

© Jason Maehl/shutterstock.com: p. 129

Photo courtesy of the U.S. Army Corps of Engineers, Office of History: p. 132

© Christa DeRidder/shutterstock.com: p. 135

© DavidKay/shutterstock.com: endpapers